Nepal – India Open Border:
Problems and Prospects

Nepal – India Open Border:
Problems and Prospects

Lok Raj Baral

Uddhab P. Pyakurel

Vij Books India Pvt Ltd

New Delhi (India)

Published by

Vij Books India Pvt Ltd
(Publishers, Distributors & Importers)
2/19, Ansari Road
Delhi – 110 002
Phones: 91-11-43596460, 91-11-47340674
Fax: 91-11-47340674
e-mail: vijbooks@rediffmail.com

Copyright © 2015, *Authors*

ISBN   : 978-93-84464-86-8 (Hardback)

ISBN   : 978-93-84464-92-9 (ebook)

All rights reserved.

No part of this book may be reproduced, stored in a retrieval system, transmitted or utilised in any form or by any means, electronic, mechanical, photocopying, recording or otherwise, without the prior permission of the copyright owner. Application for such permission should be addressed to the publisher.

The views expressed in the book are of the authors and not necessarily those of the publishers.

Supported by B.P. Koirala India-Nepal Foundation
2015

Contents

Acknowledgements		ix
Chapter I :	Background	1
Chapter II :	Nepal–India Open Border - Genesis And Dynamics	4
Chapter III :	Trade	16
Chapter IV:	The Major Issues Identified During The Fieldwork	20
Chapter V :	Border Disputes	30
Chapter VI :	Causes Behind The Border Related Problems: An Analysis	54
Chapter VII :	Conclusion, Observations And Suggestions	76
Appendices		87

Acknowledgements

A Field-based study on Nepal-India open border arrangement was long over due. When this idea was raised with the former Indian ambassador to Nepal, Shri Jayant Prasad, he promptly accepted it and went into action during the B.P. Koirala India-Nepal Foundation (BPKF) Meeting in March 2011. Yet, the project was delayed to execute due to various reasons. We are happy that the study is complete within a stipulated period of fourteen months, two more months than the term fixed by the BPKF Board. Its main reason of delay was the availability of time of Researcher, coordinator and Advisers. Since it is entirely a field-based study, visits to the field needed suitable season.

According to the original plan, two researchers, one from India and one from Nepal, were supposed to work in the project but due to his own prior commitments and job conditions, Dr. Vinod K. Bhardwaj of Jaipur, could not spare his time. Dr. Uddhab P. Pyakurel, a Nepali scholar, who teaches Political Sociology at Kathmandu University and the coordinator Professor Lok Raj Baral had to work as a full timer. Both of them have visited the field freeing themselves from their regular engagement as teacher (Uddhab), and executive head of Nepal Centre for Contemporary Studies (NCCS). Other scholars who were involved for field works were Dr. Indra Adhikari, Prof. Binaya K. Kushiyait and Bijay Raj Pant.

Ambassador of India to Nepal, Jayant Prasad, Co-Chairperson of BPKF (now retired) in particular, deserves special thanks for his interest and quick action he took for providing fund to the execution of project as well as in accepting the names of advisors and research team. His successor Ranjit Rae continued the cooperative spirit by encouraging us to hold discussion events in Patna, Lucknow and New Delhi in addition to the five meetings held in Kakarbhitta, Birgunj, Kathmandu, Bhairahawa and Mahendranagar in Nepal. We are grateful to him for taking quick decision and action. The then Acting Nepali Ambassador, K.N. Adhikari, who acted as Co-Chairman of BPKF, and the members of Board, have cooperated by gladly supporting the proposal during the BPKF Board meeting.

The Deputy Chief of Mission, Mr. Jaideep Majumdar and Mr. Abhay Kumar, (First Secretary Press, Information and Culture) of the Embassy of India deserve thanks for their cooperation. In fact, Abhay Kumar has cooperated with the team by taking quick action for releasing fund when needed. Mr. Pankaj Mallik who handled the BPKF as local staff deserves thanks for his cooperation. The two Advisors, Former Director General of SSB (India), R.K. Shukla, and former Home Secretary of Nepal, Umesh P. Mainali, have encouraged the team by accepting our request to be advisers. The suggestions made by them during our first meeting in November 2012 were valuable. While making comments on the draft of the report, Mr. Shukla provided many inputs into the subject. The report is enriched with his suggestions. We are grateful to him for taking time to come to Kathmandu for our last meeting. Ishwor Kharel and Uttam Hachhethu of NCCS deserve appreciation for their role as local logistic managers. Finally, credit goes to all the respondents, especially the SSB (India) and the APF (Nepal) personnel, local administrators of both sides, journalists and civil society members we met and discussed during the field visits.

Chapter I : Background

"Geography still counts. It counts in a strategic and tactical military sense, a political sense, and culturally defined territorial sense, and it counts in terms of the spatial distribution of resources, peoples, and physical systems"[1] .This statement is aptly correct in the context of India - Nepal Relations. Nepal's overall relations with India have been more or less determined by geographical location of the country as it faces India (South Asia) with all commonalities of the countries of the Indian subcontinent. Now this region is called South Asia and the countries of the region are integral geographical parts. Among these countries, Nepal has not only unique relationship in multiple senses as geography has destined the two countries to be together.

Going back to history, from time immemorial, both migrants and indigenous peoples inhabited the lands belonging to the northern Gangetic plain and hills. Kathmandu valley, ruled by the Newars for centuries, had its distinct cultural heritage and identity with which the King of Gorkha was infatuated. Coming as he did from a small poor hilly principality, Prithvi Narayan shah's expansion began with the ambition of becoming a king of a big empire. As his empire building expedition went on becoming successful, he and his successors extended and expanded the territories in the East and West. After conquering the Kathmandu valley fully in 1768-69, he established himself as "builder of modern Nepal". By the time Prithvi Narayan Shah died, the Gorkhali Empire was "comprised the whole of the eastern and central Tarai, inner Tarai, the whole of Kathmandu valley, and the eastern hill region up to the Tista river bordering Sikkim, with the state of Jajarkot in the north-west as a vassal".[2]

---

[1] Saul Bernard Cohen, *Geopolitics: The Geography of International Relations* (Noida, India: Pentagon Press, Indian edn, 0), p.2

[2] Mahesh C. Regimi, *Imperial Gorkha* (Delhi: Adroit publishers,1999), p.4

However, Nepal's international boundary was officially delineated only in the eighteenth century. The empire building expedition started by King Prithvinarayan Shah of Gorkha of Western Nepal and continued by his successors came to a halt after the defeat in the Anglo-Nepal war of 1815. The Treaty of Sugauli, signed in 1815 and ratified in 1816, that accepts the dictated terms of the victor, could provide Nepal with a stable international border. Some territories were ceded in 1860 after the then Prime Minister, Jang Bahadur Rana (Kunwar), established himself as credible and reliable ruler. In fact, Jang had appeased the British by taking part in quelling the Sepoy Mutiny in 1857. The mutiny, started with the aim of overthrowing the British rule, failed. It not only provided a temporary relief to the British design but also helped stabilize the Raj without any resistance. Soon thereafter, the British rulers fixed the boundary by erecting pillars in the Eastern and the Southern borders, while the Western border was divided by the Kali (Mahakali) river.

In fact, relations between India and Nepal have been close since ancient times stemming from geographical location and common ethnic, linguistic and cultural identities that overlap the two countries. Such overarching, deep and complex relations have many things to do with the border which itself is unique and unparallel in the world. In other words, the open border regime that has been in existence from time immemorial has become the most distinguishing feature of India-Nepal relations.

With this background, a research has been conducted by forming a joint research team comprising members from Nepal and India. The study, which was supported by B.P. Koirala Nepal-India Foundation, had the following objectives.

Objective of Study

Though the overall objective of the study was to understand the positive/negative dimensions of its contribution in national, regional and spatial development, the following were the specific objectives of the study.

- To analyze the open boarder provisions through realistic approach in changing context.
- To minimize the present controversies through facts.

- To document the perceptions of the real beneficiaries of the provisions.
- To explore the gaps in effective border management.
- To recommend some measures in order to manage border in a better manner.

Methodology

The team has done intense fieldwork of one year (from December 2012 to October 2013) in the bordering areas in order to collect data. Interview (the list of interviewees is available in annex) of various stakeholders of the border (security apparatus deployed in the border, governmental and non-governmental organizations working in the border, civil society members of the bordering areas, users of the border for their livelihood, users of the border for the transit purpose), and observation were the techniques applied by team to collect primary data, whereas published and unpublished reports, articles, news reports, books, blogs, etc. were the sources of secondary data.

Chapter II : Nepal-India Open Border - Genesis And Dynamics

Nepal had no fixed boundary before the signing of the Sugauli Treaty. However, psychological division seemed to work to establish political identity of both. A lot of criminal activities used to take place along the Nepal-India border before the Anglo-British war and the "criminals found a ready shelter in the territory on the other side of the border". It has been noted that "with the establishment of the Residency the prevention of the border crimes became one of the chief duties of the Resident. Unfortunately this problem had never been tackled on a formal basis, nor did the Peace Treaty (1815-16) contain any clause relating to it"[1].

Bilateral disputes that often arose along the border of states like Tirhut, Sarun and Bettiah were settled through the good offices of British Magistrate. Since many bordering states were not directly under the British rule, they often picked up border quarrels with Nepal. However, when the British Raj was already established, "the British boundary was comparatively straight and well marked by a series of pillars closely constructed, but Oudh frontier was 'sinuous to the last degree' having disconnected hills. On such a border of three hundred and fifty miles there were only six spots defined by pillars. The Treaty of Sagauli was also vague on this point. It defined the boundary by the mention of 'fist continuous line of hills, but it was well known that hills had 'no continuity'. Only after disputes were raised by either party, pillars were constructed[2]. B.H. Hodgson, then British Resident, seemed to be concerned about the border disputes occurring between Oudh and Nepal and used to draw attention of the Nepal Darbar for the reconstruction and addition of pillars. Although Nepal always agreed to solve the boundary dispute, "it refused to

---

1 Ramakant, *Indo-Nepalese Relations,1816 to 1877* (Delhi: S.Chand & Co., 1968),p.92.
2 Ibid, p. 96.

bear even half of the expense involved in regular inspection"[3].

The fallout of the defeat of the Gorkhalis in the Anglo-Gorkha war had both negative and positive consequences. Positively, after a brief spell of political instability precipitated by the court rivals and family feuds, Nepal could steer a stable course after the advent of Rana rule in 1846. Though it was family oligarchy exclusively monopolized by the Rana family members, it consolidated whatever gains Nepal could save in the Sugauli Treaty. If the British Raj could be relieved of Nepal's ambition of expansion, the latter was much assured of stability and territorial integrity as determined by the provisions of the Treaty. Since China was already a declining power, Nepal and British-India developed close relations by undertaking various measures including the demarcation of international boundary as well as making themselves as friends. Although the conclusion of the Treaty and loss of territory was a major setback to Nepal, the Treaty of Sugauli had recognized Nepal's independence and sovereignty. The Nepali king had signed the Treaty by virtue of being sovereign despite the defeat in the war. Under Article III of the Treaty, "certain territories were ceded by Nepal". It is said: The cession of territory by agreement under a peace treaty has never involved or indicated a loss of sovereignty or independence otherwise than in relation to the ceded territories. If the treaties were the case, there would be few States which could be held independent and sovereign in the present time"[4]. Losing war was one thing, maintaining sovereignty was another.

As a sovereign country, Nepal agreed to cede its territories conquered by it during the War. So "while giving away the right over Sikkim and other territories in Mechi river in the East and Kali river in the West, Nepal's king had used the prerogative of a sovereign"[5]. However, the practice of open border didn't come from the Treaty as both the peoples of Nepal and India had only psychological considerations of being different. While going over to India, Nepalis felt that they were in *Muglan* as the word *Muglan* , the land of Mugal. The white pillars (*Jange* pillars) reminded the peoples that they were entering into the foreign land. Above all, such feelings are the blood, vein and arteries of the nation state. Physical borders are only

---

[3] Foreign Political Consultation [P.C.] May 28,1830-No 19 as cited in Ramakant, ibid,p.97.

[4] See Avtar Singh Bhasin, ed., *Nepal's Relations with India and China: Documents 1947-1992*, vol.1 (Delhi: Siba Exim Pvt. Ltd. 1994),p.7.

[5] Perceval Landon, *Nepal* (London: Constable, 1928), p.101.

outward forms of national identity. Rishikesh Shaha writes:

"By the beginning of the 19th century the expansion of the Gorkhas in the hills was running parallel to that of the British in the northern and eastern parts of India, and they had evolved a common land frontier extending along a distance of at least 700 miles. The frontiers nowhere in Asia had ever been demarcated and the problem of frontiers was at its worst in India during those uncertain times when the British advances from Bengal were creating a stir in the entire region"[6].

The significance of open border was also admitted during the negotiations for retaining the Gorkha troops in the Indian Army after partition in 1947. The memorandum of Agreement between the Government of the Dominion of India and H.M. Government in the United Kingdom has stated in article 5 that "The Gorkha Officers, recruits, soldiers, ex-soldiers and pensioners, shall be permitted to travel freely between Nepal and an Indian port on their lawful occasions"[7]. Nepalese willing to join the British and Indian armies made use of the open border and travelled to different recruitment centres established in Ghoom, Darjeeling, and Gorakhpur. The very word *Lahure* (those serving the then British army) has its origin in Lahore (now in Pakistan).

It is assumed that the British rulers in India might have kept an open border between Nepal and India due to some of these reasons:

- To facilitate the Nepalese from the hilly regions to join the British army;

- To make smooth flow of British and Indian consumer goods into Nepal (economic purpose);

- To ensure free movement of timber, boulder, fire-woods herbs, hides and skin and various other raw materials ; and

- To continue the common cultural and civilization links between

---

6 Rishikesh Shaha, *Modern Nepal: A Political History, 1769-1955*, Vol.1, (Delhi: Manohar,1990), p.115.

7 See The Text in S.D. Muni, *India And Nepal: A Changing Relationship* (Delhi: Konark Publishers, 1992), p.183.

the people of Tarai and the northern plains of India[8]. This picture is now modified as all the Nepalese belonging to the hills and the Tarai have some kinds of cultural and other links with the peoples of India. The new recruits are primarily from the hill ethnic groups.

Many of the foregoing reasons are still valid. However, In Nepal today, the issue of recruitment into Indian Army has been politicized by some groups and individuals taking such an arrangement as an insult to the independent nation. Demands for ending the recruitment into foreign armies are raised even today with a committee formed by the Constituent Assembly itself seeking its abrogation. But such opinion do not go unchallenged by those who have served the foreign armies and are benefitted after their retirement and by others who want to join the Indian Army in the future. Since there is no alternative employment opportunity in the country, it is imperative for all to continue this arrangement. For India, apart from being involved in wars with other countries (non-Hindu countries), the Gorkha troops have been used as a neutral force during the grave internal crisis particularly when security situation tries to go out of hand due to inter-communal and inter-ethnic conflicts in India. In the wake of the assassination of Prime Minister, Indira Gandhi in November 1984 by her two Sikh bodyguards, for example, the Gorkha troops played a key role in Delhi to contain engulfing sectarian conflict. Now open border regime is not only a political reality, but it has cultural, demographic and historical attributes that continue even today. So far the political boundary is concerned, the two countries are separated by both semblance of demarcation pillars, tributaries, rivers and by the mental makeup that both are independent, sovereign nations with their distinct characteristics. Yet, the political demarcation does not obstruct the people to people relations despite their own legal and administrative systems for dealing with the Nepalis in India and Indians in Nepal.

As stated elsewhere, Nepal and India maintained a very unique relation which is sometimes referred to as 'special relations' too. It can be argued that some common grounds can be found in other parts of the world, but the Indo-Nepali model is found nowhere. Here are some identified features of India-Nepal border:

---

8 See Buddhi Narayan Shrestha, *Nepalko Seema (Boundary of Nepal)* (Kathmandu: Bhumichitra (Mapping) Co.pvt. Limited, 2000 , p. 278

1. It is open border as the peoples of two countries can use the border without passport, visa and other documents except those who travel by planes. However, some areas have been declared "restricted" where no foreigners including Nepalis can visit. In the past, Restricted Area Permit was needed if one wished to visit those areas in India.. Since it took a long time to obtain such permits, people used informal ways to travel. Nepalis going to Northeast India, for example, used such methods and sometimes were harassed or even deported by the Indian police.

2. It is a composite border of plain land, high hills, rivers, forests and gorges. India is on three sides, East, West and North-South. The Himalayas work as a natural barrier between Nepal and China. The original natural boundary position in the North is somewhat changed after the construction of motorable roads linking the Tibet Autonomous Region of China with Nepal. Such man-made access has changed the strategic dimension. So the Himalayas no longer stand as a natural boundary. Demand for connectivity and interactions between China, Nepal and India may further open the border. China has already constructed railways up to Sighatse in near the Kerung-Rasuwagadi along the Nepal-China border.

3. The southern border is a composite of plain land, rivers and forests. Interestingly, all Nepalese rivers flow north–south. Geography aids the natural and religious links between the two countries. Thus, rivers and the mountains including the High Himalayas have created a kind of common civilization of India and Nepal.

- Generally, no registration is needed in the border.
- It is difficult to establish one's own identity while using the border within India and Nepal.

4. Open border is regarded as a "safety-valve" for Nepal. Millions of Nepalis have been employed in India. Nepal too provides similar opportunity to Indian workers, traders and others but, given the size of India and economic capacity to absorb as many Nepalis as possible, it is considered as less problematic. However, in certain parts of India, notably in the Northeastern states, Nepalis are also not taken kindly by the local people and are forced to face deportation.

> Commonalities of language, culture, physical features (especially between the Tarai people of Nepal and northern Indians) make the open border regime more people friendly. It sometimes creates problems of national identity and national sovereignty when unscrupulous elements try to exploit the free border for self interests. Border is also used for criminal activities as it is used as a conduit for terrorists of all sorts and nationalities. It has been reported frequently in the press that criminals, armed gangs, fake currency dealers, smugglers, drug and women traffickers have been using the open borders. Now India has deployed *Seema Surakshya Bal* (SSB) on the entire Nepal-India borders. In about to four kilometer gap, the Indian armed posts have been established for the following reasons:

> Stop smuggling, movement of contraband /illegal goods, import or export without clearing custom duties

> Peace keeping, internal security and prevention of criminals from using the border

> Security of custom check points, border areas and border pillars, and prevention of trans-border crimes

> Prevention of girls trafficking

> Prevention of transaction of arms and amenities

> Prevention of transaction of fake currencies

5. Nepal too has given border duty to the Armed Police Force but due to lack of resources, it has established posts between 15-25 kilometer and even more gap.

6. It is not porous border but it can be called open border for a variety of reasons: unrestricted movement of peoples of India and Nepal; for more or less equal treatment meted out to Nepalis in India and Indians in Nepal; for continuing historical relations in political, social, economic and other fields. Although the traditional relations as determined by geography cannot alone work as obstacle to the dynamics of international relations whose impacts on the internal

and bilateral relations are no less significant, Nepal's dependency syndrome and lack of economic progress and capacity to employ its own people have not changed the pattern of bilateral relations. Nevertheless, with the changing international and regional context, Nepal-India relations seem to be evolving.

The following two aspects of Nepal-India open border have played a crucial role in remaining one of the lively aspects of Nepal-India relations.

2.1 Human Movement

Human movement is one of the major aspects of each and every international border. Due to the unique nature of the border, which provides immense economic and social opportunity, the number of peoples crossing the border for various activities both in Nepal and India is very high on daily basis. It is said that the livelihood of millions of people, living in both sides of the border, depends on that movement. It is reported that over 361 million people are living across the border in the neighbouring Indian states of Sikkim, West Bengal, Bihar, Uttar Pradesh and Uttarakhand. Due to dense habitat in both sides of the border, from morning to evening, till the closure of the activities, flocks of people pass every day making Nepal-India border one of the most dynamic and economically and socially vibrant borders of the world[9]. Since socio-cultural similarities on either side of the international border are one of the universal phenomenons, these are more pronounced in the case of Nepal-India border. According to a Nepali scholar:

> "Nepal-India border is unique in the world in the sense that people of both the countries can cross it from any point, despite the existence of border check posts at several locations. The number of check posts meant for carrying out bilateral trade is 22. However, only at six transit points out of them, the movement is permitted to nationals of third countries, who require entry and exit visa to cross the border[10]"

---

9 See, http://www.spotlightnepal.com/News/Article/The-Border-Life, accessed by authors on September1, 2013.

10 Vidya Bir Singh Kansakar "Nepal-India Open Border: Prospects, Problems and Challenges," available in http://www.nepaldemocracy.org/documents/treaties_agreements/nep_india_open_border.htm, accessed by authors on September1, 2013.

While observing cross border movement of peoples across India-Nepal border, people use this particular border on daily basis basically for some of the reasons given identified below.

2.2 Health

Most of Nepalese of different regions, especially of the border areas, go to Indian cities for medical treatment. Indians also come to Nepal for treatment in hospitals in Nepal as good facilities are provided in the Nepal Tarai hospitals in recent years. These facilities have resulted in greater inflow of eye patients from the bordering states of India because of quality and cheap services. Also hospitals like Bharatpur medical college has attracted a large number of cancer patients from India. It is equally true in the case of Nepalese. It has been observed that more than 70 percent cancer patients visit Rajiv Gandhi Cancer hospital in New Delhi. Other quality hospitals are no less attractive for the Nepalese.

2.3 Business and Livelihood

People of both the countries are involved in small and medium sized enterprises like shops across the border, whereas both Indian and Nepali laborers are actively involved in construction, agriculture, factories, and other household affairs. Tanga drivers, shops, loaders, manual workers and many other kinds of job-seekers use the open border. The Indian market provides cheaper and better quality products, encouraging the Nepalese for using such markets for daily purchases. In fact, Nepali people have been highly dependent on the Indian market across the border for their day-to-day livelihood. Most of the border markets of India are sustained only because of Nepali consumers. Even though it is not known when the open border between Nepal and India was initiated, the system of free movement of people on either side of the border started since the state formation of both sides. Indians too come to Nepalese side for entertainment purpose as very many Bars and Restaurants including Casinos are available in the bordering cities of Nepal. The open border and its own historical and contemporary significance for both countries is very important in understanding Flow of skilled labourers from India and unskilled manpower from Nepal is also a common feature.

2.4. Education

It is difficult to trace exactly when Nepali students started going to India for education. However, it is said that India has been an educational hub for the Nepalese ever since the Gurukul system of education started. The trend accelerated with the advancement in the education system after the initiation of formal education some 200 years ago. The flow of Nepali students to the neighbouring country kept on rising since the days of the Rana regime when education used to be the exclusive prerogative of the ruling elite and then beneficiaries. Today, those who could afford send their children to various places in India. There are many popular destinations such as Darjeeling, Kurseong, Kalimpong, Nainital, Dehradun and Mussorie for school education. Other big cities are increasingly becoming attractive for higher studies. It is said that some 500,000 students are studying in Indian schools[11], and it is being continued due to schools in Nepal which could not deliver the "quality education compared to those in the neighbouring country". Adoption of tight visa rules for students in The United States, the United Kingdom and Australia, India is a proximate destination for Nepal. And people make a choice as India is affordable for middle class people. Similar cultures of both the countries are identified as other factors making India as a secure destination for Nepalese children's higher education[12]. Apart from these general trends, many Indian students are now taking their education in medical science in the bordering cities of Nepal. Today, there are 20 medical colleges, and many of them are located in Nepal's Tarai. These medical colleges have attracted a large number of Indian students seeking medical education and also patients seeking medical services in these hospitals. The attraction towards study of medicine in Nepal is also due to the cost involved apart from the quality of education.

2.5 Transit

Nepalese travelling to third countries through India have also increased the frequency of movement across the border. Though the number of people travelling through different points is diverse, a good number of Nepalese

---

11 See, http://www.myrepublica.com/portal/index.php?action=news_details&news_id=60148, accessed by authors on September1, 2013.

12 http://www.ekantipur.com/2013/06/13/national/india-the-most-preferred-destination-for-nepali-students/373181.html

citizens cross the border point for transit purpose. According to a report[13], 400 to 500 migrant workers are flying to Gulf countries on a daily basis from Indian airports. It is claimed that around 100 to 150 Nepali workers fly to third countries through Lucknow and Delhi alone. Though avoiding unnecessary hassles at the Nepali airport is one of the major reasons for this choice, lack of embassies of the destination countries in Nepal, flying costs, legal hassles and the lack of a proper monitoring mechanism are other reasons for Nepalis travelling overland to India. "It is mostly people working in India and those living near the Indian border who are travelling through Indian airports. As we do not have the embassies of any of the destination countries, except Malaysia, workers find it easier to obtain visas and leave from India,"[14]

The entry and exit of nationals from the third countries is another cause of the frequency of movement across the border. There are six immigration points (Banbasa, Dhangadhi, Nepalganj, Bhairahawa (Sunauli), Birganj and Kakarvitta) along the Indo Nepal border for the entry and exit of nationals from third countries, and thousands of third country tourists take these routes while travelling to both the countries.

2.6 Family Relations

Large numbers of families across the border are tied through marital relations. So apart from the very specific reasons for movement, people generally go across the border to see their families, friends and relatives.

2.7 Migration (seasonal and permanent)

Open border facilitated -migration (seasonal and permanent) seems to be the driving force for human movement in the border. Studies (Thieme 2006:1) state that there could be 1.3 to 3 million Nepalese working in India. This figure is higher now as Nepalese have reached almost all places, particularly town and cities. During insurgency period (1996-2005) and forced by natural calamities and lack of employment, Nepalese go to India for immediate redemption. In other words, there is huge number of cross border migration between Nepal and India. The following causes are

---

13 Roshan Sedhai, "Worries as more migrant workers leaving via India", *The Kathmandu Post*, September 11, 2012.

14 Kumud Khanal, as cited in *The Kathmandu Post*, Ibid.

identified for such migration.

2.8 To avoid conflict

Avoiding conflict in home or destination country is one of the major causes of Nepal-India migration. The number of people crossing over the border to India through certain border checkpoints shot up to 2,000 per day during the conflict period[15]. From the Nepalganj sector alone, the number of people crossing over the border from Nepal to India was 300 to 400 per day in November-December 2002, which shot up unprecedentedly to 1,200 during the same period in 2003[16]. During the conflict period 24,000 people from the Rajapur areas of the Bardiya district had left their villages *en masse* to settle in the Baharaich and nearby areas across the border in India[17].

According to a recent report, some 25 per cent workers in the construction sector in Nepal are Indian, whereas Indian shares more than 75 per cent in ornament business. Also, it is estimated that 40-50 per cent Indian workers are in tailoring and garment industries, and the similar portion of Indians are working in Nepal as street venders. The report reveals that some 50 thousand workers from Rajasthan are living in Nepal in order to work on marble and tile area. It has been identified that out of all labourers who all the way come to Nepal for job, only 10 per cent have brought their family members together with them. Also of those workers, some 20 per cent Indians are living in Nepal for more than 20 years while working, whereas some 40 per cent are living in Nepal for 5 years and the rest are mobile labourers who often go and come[18]. Since the big numbers

---

15 for details, see www.ipsnews.co.th/writingpeace/features/nepal.html; see also Hari Bansa Jha, "Economics of Conflict and Peace with focus on Nepal", a paper submitted to a seminar "New Dynamics of Development: Challenges and Prospects" organized by Centre for Economic and Technical Studies (CETS) In cooperation with Friedrich-Ebert-Stiftung (FES), 12 & 13 November 2008.

16 Save the Children – Norway, "A Study on Impacts of Armed Conflict Pushing Girls and Women into Sexual Abuse and Sex Trade" (Kathmandu, 2005)

17 Bishnu Raj Upreti, "Environmental Stress and Armed Conflict: A Study on Effects of Maoist Insurgency on Environmental Sanitation and Health of Internally Displaced Persons of Urban Areas of Kathmandu City of Nepal" (paper submitted to International Conference on Health and Environmental Research Challenges in *Urban Poor Settlement*, organized by Swiss Centre for Scientific Research in Côte d'Ivoire, September 3-5,2005), 4.

18 Sujit Mahat and Roshan Adhikari, "Earnings of Foreign Workers is Higher than the

of Indian laborers working in Nepal are quite mobile, it obviously helps to make Nepal-India border busy. Also, those who live longer in Nepal while working, invite their family members and friends in Nepal not only for family affairs but also for pilgrimage visits, trekking, etc.

Workers went Abroad", *Kantipur*, September 9, 2013.

Chapter III : Trade

Nepal Depends on India for trade as the latter's goods need to pass through India transit point. Nepal-India border has the following 22 designated trade routes:

Table 1: Agreed routes for Mutual Trade by Nepal and India

	Agreed routes for Mutual Trade
1.	Pashupatinagar / Sukhia Pokhari
2.	Kakarbhitta / Naxalbari
3.	Bhadrapur / Galgalia
4.	Biratnagar / Jogbani
5.	Setubandha / Bhimnagar
6.	Rajbiraj / Kunauli
7.	Siraha, Janakpur / Jayanagar
8.	Jaleswar / Bhitamode(Sursand)
9.	Malangawa / Sonbarsa
10.	Gaur / Bairgania
11.	Birgunj / Raxaul
12.	Bhairahawa / Nautanwa
13.	Taulihawa / Khunwa
14.	Krishnanagar / Barhni
15.	Koilabas / Jarwa
16.	Nepalgunj / Nepalgunj Road
17.	Rajapur / Katerniyaghat

18.	Prithivipur / Sati (Kailali) / Tikonia
19.	Dhangadhi / Gauriphanta
20.	Mahendranagar / Banbasa
21.	Mahakali / Jhulaghat (Pithoragarh)
22.	Darchula/Dharchula

Source: Department of Customs, HMG/Nepal

Out of 22, the following 15 have been specified for Nepal's third-country imports/exports trade.

1. Sukhia pokhari
2. Naxalbari (Panitanki)
3. Galgalia
4. Jogbani
5. Bhimnagar
6. Jayanagar Road, Rail (NG)
7. Bhitamode Road
8. Raxaul Road, Rail (BG)
9. Nautanwa (Suneuali) Road
10. Barhni Road
11. Jarwa Road
12. Nepalgunj Road, Road
13. Tikonia Road
14. Gauriphanta Road
15. Banbasa Road

For Nepal's third country trade, Kolkata and Haldia on the eastern coast of India have been specified. Kolkata port has a` draft limitation of 7.2

metres depending upon the tide. A slightly more draft of up to 10 metres is available at Haldia port. Nepal has proposed some more access ports in both the East and West coasts. Deep seaports can accommodate large ships[1]. In order to facilitate the trade, Government of India is providing assistance for development of cross-border trade related infrastructure. It includes upgradation of four major custom checkpoints at Birgunj-Raxaul, Biratnagar-Jogbani, Bhairahawa-Sunauli and Nepalgunj-Rupaediya to international standards; upgrading approach highways to the border on the Indian side; upgrading and expanding the road network in the Tarai region of Nepal; and, broad gauging and extending rail links to Nepal. Also, India and Nepal signed a Rail Services Agreement (RSA) in May 2004, to extend cargo train service to the Inland Container Depot (ICD) at Birgunj in Nepal. A Container Corporation of India-led joint venture is operating the ICD. The RSA was modified in December 2008 to allow oil/liquid traffic in tank wagons and bilateral break-bulk cargo in flat wagons.

It is stated that bilateral trade was US$ 4.21 billion during Nepalese fiscal year 2010-11 (July 16 – July 15). Nepal's import from India amounted to US$ 3.62 billion and exports to India aggregated US$ 599.7 million. In the first six months of fiscal year 2011-12, Nepal's total trade with India was about US$ 1.93 billion; Nepal's exports to India were about US$ 284.8 million; and imports from India were about US$ 1.64 billion. Since 1996, Nepal's exports to India have grown more than eleven times and bilateral trade more than ten times; the bilateral trade that was 29.8 per cent of total external trade of Nepal in year 1995-96 has increased to 66.4 per cent in 2010-11. Since 1995-96, the total external trade of Nepal has increased from NRs. 9433 crores (IRs.5895 crores) to NRs. 45946.1 crores (IRs. 28716.3 crores). 83 per cent of this increase is on account of increase in the bilateral trade between India and Nepal, which grew from NRs. 2808 crores (IRs. 1755 crores) in 1995-96 to NRs. 16319.9 crores (IRs. 10199.9 crores) in first six months of 2011-12. Nepal's exports also increased from NRs.1988 crores (IRs. 1242 crores) in 1995-96 to NRs. 3591.6 crores (IRs. 2244.7 crores) in first six months of 2011-12. 45 per cent of this increase was on account of increase in Nepal's exports to India. According to the official website of Indian Embassy to Nepal, Nepal's main imports from India are petroleum products (28.6%), motor vehicles and spare parts (7.8%), M. S. billet (7%), medicines (3.7%), other machinery and spares

---

1 Sanjib Pohit, "Overview of India-Nepal Trade: Trends, Trade Logistics and Impediments", MPRA Paper No. 45874, 2009.

(3.4%), coldrolled sheet in coil (3.1%), electrical equipment (2.7%), hot rolled sheet in coil (2%), M. S. wires, roads, coils and bars (1.9%), cement (1.5%), agriculture equipment and parts (1.2%), chemical fertilizer (1.1%), chemicals (1.1%) and thread (1%). Nepal's export basket to India mainly comprises jute goods (9.2%), zinc sheet (8.9%), textiles (8.6%), threads (7.7%), polyster yarn (6%), juice (5.4%), catechue (4.4%), Cardamom (4.4%), wire (3.7%), tooth paste (2.2%) and M.S. Pipe (2.1%).

One can classify trade related activities of Nepal-India border in two broad categories, which are:

- *Formal Trade*: Trade conducted through the proper channels and with valid documentations. The data presented above relate to the formal trade.

- *Informal Trade:* It is the trade which occurs without any documentation. It can be big by carrying in a small quantity. It is reported that Nepal-India's informal trade is much higher than what is officially registered. According to a report[2], nearly 55 per cent people along the Nepal-India border region conduct border trade for private consumption, 23 per cent for business purposes and the remaining 14 per cent for social functions. It is said that about 68 per cent of the border inhabitants use authorized custom checkpoints for border trade, while the remaining one third go for trade through non-custom checkpoints. Though it is difficult to go for any estimate about the volume of border trade between Nepal and India, it is estimated that each day there is a transaction of around 50 million rupees worth of goods through only the Sunauli border[3]. The total value of informal imports of agricultural products from India to Nepal amounted to Rs. 55 billion in 2012[4].

---

2   Hari Bansh Jha, "Nepal's Border Relations with India and China", available in http://www.borderstudies.jp/en/publications/review/data/ebr4/V4_N1_04Jha.pdf, accessed on September 6, 2013.

3   "Traders Block Nepal Border in Maharajgunj," http://articles.timesofindia.indiatimes.com/2012-09-30/ lucknow/34177269_1_indo-nepal-border-nepal-india-peace-nepals-maoist-party.

4   https://plus.google.com/110700033722522182284/posts/TLpc3WCkyWW

Chapter IV: The Major Issues Identified During The Fieldwork

The following section discuses some of the major issues identified during the fieldwork. As mentioned earlier, the study team visited 19 different points of the Nepal-India border (the details are available in the annex) starting from Pashupatinagar of Ilam / Darjeeling of India in the Eastern border to Dharchula/Mangalsen in the West. Though there are some specific issues and characters of some of the border points, the general issues related to Nepal-India border are mainly human trafficking, cross-border crime, smuggling or illegal trade, border disputes or issue of encroachment, lack of coordination among and between the agencies deployed in the border by Nepal and India, issue of insufficient access to Indian Currency, issue of harassment of commoners by the border security forces, nexus between security agencies and local mafia, issue of Noman's land, mismanagement and disappearance of border pillars, issue of poor infrastructure in the border, complications due to the lack of uniform legal system in the bordering areas, complications due to the inequality among the people residing in bordering areas, anti-India drive by Nepalese leadership, etc. Broadly speaking, the above identified problems can be classified in four categories that have been dealt with separately in the following sections.

4.1 Smuggling or Illegal Trade

The general meaning of smuggling is import or export without paying lawful customs charges or duties. It is said that unauthorized trade is common almost all through the border points, including in the Kakarbhitta, Biratnager, Janakpur, Birgunj, Bhairahawa and Nepalganj corridors. Often, the carriers involved in unauthorized trade load goods either on their heads or on bicycles while crossing over the border. According to a report[1] about

---

1   Hari Bansh Jha, "Nepal's Border Relations with India and China", available in http://

68 per cent of the border inhabitants of Nepal-India border use authorized custom checkpoints for border trade, while the remaining one third go for trade through non-custom checkpoints.

In fact, many of the farmers living along the border regions buy and sell agricultural and livestock products at the border *hat bazaars* and other market centres in each other's territory. The Nepalese border inhabitants buy commodities i.e. sugar, food grains, clothes, cooking oil, cement, fertilizers, electrical and electronic goods to meet their daily needs at the neighbouring markets of Bengal, Bihar, Uttar Pradesh and Uttarakhand of India. Such goods of daily needs are relatively cheaper in India than in Nepal. The Indian border inhabitants, however, buy such goods in Nepal that originate from third countries like China, Japan, Thailand, Hong Kong, Singapore and Taiwan. There is also unauthorized trade in gold, *Supari* (betelnut), and tea from Nepal to India. As mentioned in earlier sections, nearly 55 per cent of the peoples along the Nepal-India border region conduct border trade for private consumption, and 14 per cent for social functions. The border inhabitants who buy goods for their household needs across the border do not want to pay customs. A good number of the carriers involved in unauthorized trade load goods either on their heads or on bicycles while crossing over the border. Such carrier service is found in the cities which are some 15 Kilometres away from the border, and many children, women and other abled people are used in this activity.

Apart from them, peoples from bordering districts also come to the bordering markets to buy goods for their household needs. We have met people who came from 100 Kilometres away to buy goods for their household needs. And people (mostly Nepalese) travel a long way (even up to 200 Kilometres) to buy goods if there are social functions like marriage, death anniversary etc. Two major causes are clear for such border trade movement of peoples; the first is due to the cost benefit. Some goods are really cheaper than in the other sides of border and hence temptation to buy goods increases. Sometimes people want to make this opportunity as part of their outing activities. They know that they are not getting these goods in cheaper price if all the costs (i.e. travel expenses, money spent for tea and snacks, etc. on the way) are added. More so, psychology also works. Discussion with Santosh Agrawal, a Rajasthani origin businessmen

---

www.borderstudies.jp/en/publications/review/data/ebr4/V4_N1_04Jha.pdf, accessed on September 6, 2013.

doing business in Dhangadi bazaar was eye opening for us. "People travel all the way to Indian market to buy goods which are available cheaper in Nepali market. They have a feeling that it is Indian product and should be cheaper there. But this is not the case always" he stated[2]. According to him, the goods are sold in Indian market as per the printed Maximum Retail Price (MRP), whereas Nepali dealers get the same thing in wholesale rate.

Apart from these commodities which are bought and sold for daily household purposes, restricted or internationally banned items i.e. hashish, several medicinal herbs and body parts of wild animals, endangered species, endangered mammal, contraband firearms and ammunitions, red sandalwood, etc. are also found smuggled by using Nepal-India borders. The racketeers, who are directly involved in all such activities, have started using people from vulnerable community in such works. Tulsi Sunar of Ghorahi, Dang, seems to be the one case one of such cases. Sunar a Dalit woman was caught by SSB with 4 kilograms of hashish from Jamunah, Rupaediya. According to media reports, she was asked by someone (Jyoti Magar of Dang) to smuggle the goods to New Delhi, India[3]. Nabi Alam, a reporter of Jana Sandesh, states that there are some 110 Nepalese women in Baharaich jail of Uttar Pradesh for their involvement in smuggling hashish. They are spending difficult life in jail due to allurement of a little amount of money. According to Alam, most of them are from Western Hills of Nepal who were arrested in border points while smuggling hashish from various districts of mid-western region[4]. Though it is the case of Jamunaha point of Banke's border and Murtiya of Bardiya, similar cases are reported in other border points as well.

Here, we need to discuss why the involvement of vulnerable community i.e. women, and children has being increased in smuggling business in the bordering areas. It was one of the questions we have asked to those who were busy in carrying goods for business purpose. Answer of a lady who was hiding behind the tree in order to wait for a favourable situation to cross the Gaurifanta border point seems to be quite interesting. According to her, if there is male involved in carrying business, he will be

---

2 As per discussion with researchers, January 2, 2013.

3 For details, see http://ekantipur.com/2013/09/23/top-story/indian-ssb-arrest-nepali-woman-from-rupediya-border/378394.html, accessed by the author on September 24, 2013.

4 Researchers' discussion with him on December 29, 2012.

beaten up and even jailed by the security which is not the case for women and children. "That is why we are in majority in the bordering areas", she states. She also disclosed the fact that the border management agency is not that much inhuman in stopping them. "I have already crossed the border point with some goods and materials in the morning. While doing so, I was told by security not to come again today. That is why I am here to wait the time of their duty shift. Once the duty person is changed, I will be allowed once more", she stated. In a way, one may extend his/her sympathy towards the poor and say that the vulnerable groups residing in the border should be allowed to earn their livelihood by allowing them to carry goods and materials. But while having this position, one has to be cautious about the long-term social impact on that particular community. Interestingly, only a few people explained about the social impact of such carrying and smuggling activities in the local level. Mani Ram Sharma[5], a teacher and social activist in Rupaediya, states that people's involvement in carrying business has negative impact on the society. He states: People left thinking about serious work as they easily earn a handsome amount by carrying a couple of bags of grains, sugar and etc. Since a child can earn money at the age of 7-8, why should their parents send them to school? Since they get more money than Government Scheme, why should villagers work with government? As a result, neither students are in school, nor is there labour available in government projects like Mahatma Gandhi Rural Employment Guarantee Scheme (MGREGS). On the one hand the child who started carriers' business is likely to be converted into a criminal in the future, the government programmes i.e. MGREGS remained in paperwork on the other.

4.2 Cross-border crime, including Fake Currency Issue

Cross-border crime is another issue identified in the Nepal-India border. It is said that the presence of criminal groups in the border region is an enormous security challenge for both the countries. There is also argument that unregulated border enables the criminal groups to cross the border to evade police action. On the one hand, the Ministry of Home Affairs of Government of Nepal, discloses saying that there are around 109 armed groups active in Nepal out of which the majorities are based in the Tarai

---

5   As per discussion with researchers on December 30. 2012.

(bordering areas) region.[6] Abduction, kidnapping, extortion, trafficking in fake currency, drugs, small arms and persons, are reported as the main activities of such criminal groups. On the other, India has shown its concern about "increased madrasas in the border region". According to Director General of Sashastra Seema Bal (SSB), Tilak Kak, around 1900 Madrasas have come up in the border region and security agencies are monitoring the activities of fifty or sixty "sensitive" ones among them. According to Nayak (2011), along with such growth and Inter Service Intelligence (ISI) involvement, it is said that the border has become a major hub for trafficking in fake currency, small arms, drugs and persons. It is estimated that around Rs 1690 billion worth of fake currency is in circulation all over India, and in many cases Nepal-India border has been used[7].

4.3. Human Trafficking

Apart from illegal trade, cross-border crime and smuggling, the open border has the problem of heinous crime of human trafficking. Trafficking in persons is both a global phenomenon and one of the most prevalent crimes of the modern world. It takes a heavy toll of hundreds of thousands of victims annually, and indiscriminately affects stable democracies, countries in transition, and societies immersed in war. International organizations, governments, and non-governmental groups have recognized human trafficking as a contemporary form of slavery and in certain circumstances a crime against humanity[8].

4.3.1 Scope and Nature of Trafficking

The scope of human trafficking from Indo-Nepal border is difficult to ascertain due to lack of reliable statistical information, open and highly congested border with India and the clandestine nature of the crime[9].

---

6 Narayan Manandhar, "Nepal's armed groups", *Republica*, August 29, 2009, http://www.myrepublica.com/portal/index.php?action=news_details&news_id=9156, accessed by authors on September 24, 2013.

7 Nihar Nayak , " Open Border Security Challenges for India" , unpublished paper presented to a two-day seminar on The 60th Year of 1950 India-Nepal Treaty, held in Kathamandu on 11-12 September 2010.

8 American Bar Association, "HUMAN TRAFFICKING ASSESSMENT TOOL REPORT FOR NEPAL", 2011, available in http://www.americanbar.org/content/dam/aba/directories/roli/nepal/nepal_human_trafficking_assessment_report_2011.authcheckdam.pdf, accessed by the authors on September 21, 2013.

9 M. Hennink and P. Simkhada, *Sex Trafficking in Nepal: Context and Process*.

The Major Issues Identified During The Fieldwork

Human trafficking occurs both internally and trans-nationally and manifests itself through many hidden pockets, which have not been explored and addressed thoroughly. It is a highly complex, cross-cutting issue interlinked with poverty, unemployment, gender discrimination, social exclusion, globalization, internal displacement, and foreign migration[10]. Yet, it is often simplified and addressed as a standalone matter rather than being mainstreamed into the country's leading development plans and policies. The major forms of trafficking in persons in Nepal are associated with the following forms of exploitation:

- Sexual exploitation of Nepali women and girls abroad (particularly in India) and domestically (particularly within the hospitality and entertainment industries);

- Exploitation of Nepali migrant workers (particularly in the Gulf States and Malaysia);

- Exploitation of Nepali children in Indian circuses;

- Worst forms of child labour;

- Illicit organ transplantation.

Maiti Nepal has been actively working in bordering areas for 14 years. They have mobilized 4-10 border guards to monitor and check human trafficking in Nepal-India border. Various awareness campaigns as well as coordinating works have been major focus during the recent years to reduce the number of women and girls being trafficked every day through the border. Also, "anti-trafficking group" formations have been effective in raising awareness as well as monitoring activities in the border. Apart from Maiti Nepal, there are other three organizations currently working in anti-trafficking field. Organisations like *Sana Hath Haru, KI Nepal, Bikash Development* have joined hands with Maiti Nepal in their cause. Each organization has its own booths closer to each other, with a purpose of getting hold of human traffickers. In cases trafficker manages to escape the first booth, he may be caught in the subsequent booths. The number of

---

Opportunities and Choices, Paper 11, 2004.

10 American Bar Association, "HUMAN TRAFFICKING ASSESSMENT TOOL REPORT FOR NEPAL", 2011, available in http://www.americanbar.org/content/dam/aba/directories/roli/nepal/nepal_human_trafficking_assessment_report_2011.authcheckdam.pdf, accessed by the authors on September 21, 2013.

trafficking however has decreased significantly after the emergence of the above organizations in the border areas. Maiti Nepal revealed that increased awareness among the people has led to decrease in the number of women and girls being sold in India. As per the data provided by Maiti Nepal, 37 women and girls were rescued from the border alone by Maiti Nepal in the year 2011, whereas the number decreased to 12 by the year 2012. Currently, in 2013 three cases have been filed in the month of February and March. However, the major challenge faced today is trafficking to the third country via Indian route. It has posed yet another problem in the scenario of human trafficking. Moreover, boy child are also trafficked in large number to Bombay who are used by the gangs to sell *chatpate*, coconut and also use in embroidery works.

In cases where the traffickers are caught along with the victims in the border areas, they are interviewed in separate rooms ensuring their involvement in the human trafficking. Once it is confirmed, they are sent to headquarters where necessary legal action is taken. The traffickers are sentenced to 10 years of imprisonment. Most of the females are sent back to their villages and in cases where they prefer to stay at Maiti Nepal, they are given several vocational trainings, helping them to get involved in income generating activities. Women are also increasingly seen to be involved in trafficking of females as it is easier for them to gain trust from female victims. Traffickers spend as much as NPR 10,000 on the victims and sell for as much as NPR 150,000 if sold in third countries. At the same time, provision of intense punishments by the government has been successful in making the perpetrators alert.

4.3.2 How does it work ?

If preventive measures fail, Maiti Nepal sometimes manages to intercede to free girls from brothels. Rescued girls are housed in transit home, located in the border town Birgunj, where a little vigilance can have significant payoffs. They provide safe shelter as well as counselling, medical check-ups and non-formal education classes to rescued girls and write up the history and profile of each, trace parents or guardians and arrange reunions, identify and file criminal cases against traffickers and work with police to intercept potential victims and apprehend criminals. Rescued girls have formed surveillance teams which have been instrumental in helping police identify criminals and have served as a major deterrent to trafficking.

They also raise public awareness and mobilize concerned citizens to fight against trafficking. Requests for help to locate missing girls, rescue girls from brothels and provide legal advice in cases of domestic violence and polygamy number about six or seven every week in each transit house.

4.3.3 Implementation

Our observation however showed that the works being done at the border was not much effective. During the observation of almost 2 hours, no rickshaws or any other vehicles, or any people were checked by the border guards at the booths. Although we crossed the border several times, no one raised any question on our movement. This shows the need for more effective and strict implementation of inspections by the border security guards. More staffs can be recruited who would work on shift basis so that perpetrator would not be able to flee easily by crossing the border.

Facts

- Intercepted two hundred and ninety one (291) children and women at the border.
- Informed fifteen thousand, seven hundred and ninety three (15,793) migrants on safe migration procedures.
- Settled eighteen (18) cases of gender violence in favour of the survivors.
- Registered one (01) trafficking case in district court. One trafficker is in police custody awaiting trial, three are absconding.
- Traced and reunited twenty five (25) of the sixty nine (69) girls reported missing with their families.
- Inspected four thousand three hundred and twenty two (4,322) vehicles crossing the border, providing occupants with information on safe migration.
- Rescued and repatriated four (04) children and women from India. One girl was rescued from Betiya, Uttar Pradesh; another girl was rescued from Kolkatta, West Bengal; and two girls were liberated from Delhi.
- Provided short term shelter for thirty seven (37) children and women referred to the transit home by the VDCs, other organizations and the women's cell of police.
- Showed tele-documentary "Chhori" to more than 1000 people in Birgunj, Belwa and Thori.
- On the occasion of 100 International Women Day, a rally for
- 800 persons were organized; participants also recited the poems on problems faced by women.
- An orientation program on role of security personnel in combating trafficking was organized for 28 participants of police, armed police and army.
- Conducted orientation sessions reaching 293 school students of six schools at Thori, Nirmalbasti, Birwagothi and Belahawa VDC's.
- Organized a meeting for 33 media personnel to update them on work of the transit home.

Source: Maiti Nepal, Birganj

Chapter V : Border Disputes

5.1. Border Security

The security of international border is taken as a serious concern by respective governments. Border and check points are most sensitive areas because of their importance in human movement and trade transaction. Protecting borders from the illegal movement of weapons, drugs, contrabands, and people, while promoting lawful entry and exit, are considered essential to every country's security, economic prosperity, and national sovereignty.

As for Nepal, there were no security personnel deployed in Nepal-India border till recently. In the wake of intense pressure from the Maoist insurgency since 1996, Nepal declared State of Emergency in 2001. As a follow up of this decision, Nepal had deputed 410 Nepal Army personnel in 12 Customs Offices and 89 Sub-Customs points of Tarai from 14 March 2001. But the primary objective of the Army deputation was not for border patrolling, but for providing security to custom officials.

Eventually the Nepal Government decided to deploy a special wing of APF which is known as *Sasastra Prahari Seema Surkshya Bal* in 20 districts of Tarai on 5 March 2007. The objective of this was for border security as well as for plugging up revenue leakage. All together 9,000 APF personnel had been deployed in 22 Seema Surakshya Karyalaya[1], 48 Border out -Posts (BoPs) and 25 temporary security posts of Nepal-India and Nepal -China borders (Armed Police Day Special Publication, 2012. pp. 41-42)[2].

As far as India's Security Apparatus in the Nepal-India border is concerned, it has assigned Shashastra Seema Bal (SSB), a Border Guarding

---

1   Out of 22 Karyalayas, 20 are in Tarai (Nepal-India border), and the remaining two are in Nepal-China bordering districts.

2   http://www.apf.gov.np/document/publication2069.pdf

Force (BGF) under the administrative control of the Indian Ministry of Home Affairs, for border's overall security in Indian sides of Nepal-India border. Though it was set up in early 1963 in the wake of the Sino-Indian War, it was deployed in different parts of India i.e. the then North Eastern Frontier Area (NEFA), North Bengal (northern areas of West Bengal state), hills of Uttar Pradesh, Himachal Pradesh, and Ladakh to inculcate the feelings of national belonging in the border population and to develop their capabilities for resistance through a continuous process of motivation, training, development, welfare programmes and activities. The SSB was declared and deployed as a border guarding force and lead intelligence agency (LIA) for Indo-Nepal border since January, 2001, following the recommendations of the Group of Ministers on reforming the National Security System. The roles of the SSB according to its official website (http://ssb.nic.in) are as follows:

➢ To promote sense of security among the people living in the border area

➢ To Prevent trans border crimes and unauthorized entries into or exit from the territory of India

➢ To prevent smuggling and other illegal activities

According to SSB, it has covered the following area of Nepal-India border.

Table 3: Coverage area of SSB, India in Nepal-India border

Sl. No.	State	Total border length (in Kms)
1	Uttarakhand	263
2	Uttar Pradesh	560
3	Bihar	729
4	West Bengal	100
5	Sikkim	99
6	Total	1,751

Source: SSB Official Website, http://ssb.nic.in.

The initial strength of the SSB in 2001 was 25 Bahini (brigade), which increased in 2010 by 43 and it will be 73 shortly. Since 2004, it has been given responsibility to guard India-Bhutan border as well. As far as its vigilance is concerned, India has 450 Border out- Posts (BoPs) along the Indo-Nepal border and has deputed 15-25 SSB in each post. The distance between two BoPs is about 4.5 km. According to the new security strengthening plan of India for the Nepal border, over the next five years, 89 new BoPs will be created and the aim is to reduce the inter-BoP distance to 3.47 km.

Though some people had shown anxiety over the deployment of Para-military forces from both the sides in the Nepal-India border saying that two lions cannot remain in one jungle[3], the deployment of SSB and APF has significantly reduced crimes of robbery in border regions. Incidents of robbery in bordering areas have gone down after the presence of SSB and APF. The security forces on both sides are entrusted with duties for:

➢ Stopping

➢ smuggling, the movement of contraband /illegal goods, import or export without clearing custom duties

➢ Peace keeping, internal security and prevention of criminals from passing the border

➢ Security of custom check points, border areas and border pillars,and and prevention of trans-border crimes

➢ Prevention of girls trafficking

➢ Prevention of transaction of arms and amenities

➢ Prevention of transaction of fake currencies

In addition to the Special Forces deployed especially to look after border security, there are many line agencies available in the border. Immigration offices, Custom offices, Custom Agents Association, Civilian police forces, intelligence agencies, quarantine offices, anti-human trafficking cells of the Indian police, non-governmental organizations i.e. Maiti Nepal, working against human trafficking, etc. are found working in the bordering areas. On top of these, Border District Coordination Committee (BDCC) comprising all government authorities are deployed by both the countries in the Nepal-India border. It is a district level joint body which will be led

---

3   See, Buddhi Narayan Shrestha "Guarding Indo-Nepal border", October 28th, 2006, available at http://www.kiratisaathi.com/blog.php?id=78

by Chief District Officer (CDO) from Nepal side and District Magistrate (DM) of Indian side. Initially, the two countries reached an agreement to hold such meeting as and when required in order to sort out the problems seen in the bordering areas at local level. The BDCC meeting was given responsibility to oversee if missing border pillers, maintain the pillars and take necessary measures to disallow encroachment in the 'no man's land'.

However, in 2014 teams of Home Secretaries of both India and Nepal agreed to hold Border District BDCC meetings every three months on a regular basis. It is said that the meeting discussed ways to curb cross border crimes, human trafficking, fake Indian currency smuggling, trafficking of narcotics and psychotropic substances across the Indo-Nepal border, and has given emphasis on effective coordination and exchange of information at ground level between APF and its Indian counterpart SSB along the bordering districts. Also, it is reported that the two sides reached an agreement to appoint one nodal officer each at the District Administration Office, Border Security Posts, and District Police Office in all bordering districts to share intelligence information with their counterparts on real time basis. The appointment of nodal officers is expected to effectively curb crime along the border, enabling police personnel on both sides of the border to act promptly[4]. The idea to exchange of information at ground level seems to be very useful to resolve Nepal-India border related issues. During our field work, almost all government officials from both the countries referred to the BDCC and said that they have started resolving many local problems on the spot at the local level through the meeting. However, since there was no strict rule to meet, and it was provisioned saying "as and when required", CDOs and DMs were given flexibility. That is why many cases are pending due to the lack of BDCC meetings for months. Once there is no compulsion, they always have another priority, and with some pretexts they used to postpone the meeting. Some of the Nepalese CDOs told us that they could not organize meeting due to lack of budget. Along with this step, there is a great hope that the BDCC meet in every three months and resolve all border related problems at the local level.

---

4   Kosh Raj Koirala, "Nepal, India to share intelligence in real time", *The Republica*, June 4, 2013.

5.2. Dams, Barrage and Disturbance in Border

High dams, barrage along the India-Nepal border gets prominence in newspaper reports in Nepal almost regularly. Problem of inundation of lands closer to the dam sites and concomitant steps that need to be taken for mitigating this problem seems to give grounds to unnecessary controversy. Apart from big barrage such as Koshi, Gandak and Sharada, many other smaller dam projects built by India on its side have generated controversies or even making it a permanent feature of Nepal-India relation.

Problems of inundation by dams and barrages constructed by India within its territory, but close to the Nepal-India border, are the regular features of Nepali press. Among the most controversial among the High and small dams are Koshi, Gandak, Bairgania circular dam near Gaur,Rautahat, Russiawal-Khurda-Lotan Dam near the Rupandehi district India-Nepal border, Mahalisagar dam near Kapilbastu border, Laxmanpur Dam close to the Banke –India Nepal border, Sharada barrage On Mahakali river, proposed Pancheswar dam on the Mahakali near Dadeldhura and Baitadi and, Dhauliganga dam near Darchula are some of the frequently mentioned dams and barrages. The main gist of the controversy is the inundation of Nepali lands near the border and the floods caused by the opening of gates during the monsoon when the rivers are swollen. In 2013 June, it had been alleged that opening of gates of the Dhauliganga tributary of the Mahakali was responsible for causing damage to the Nepali side. However, the Indian embassy refuted such allegation maintaining that since the Dhauliganga project was built on the run off the river system and waters flowing in the river were released as in any other running river waters, such damages were done on both Indian and Nepali side. Moreover, the intensity of flood effects might have been more due to lack of stone-walled embankment on the Nepali side of the Mahakali river. The intensity of flashfloods in Uttarakhand of India was unprecedented in 2013 taking thousands of lives, sweeping away the roads and building built near the big rivers that form the Ganges. The extent of damage done by the flash flood on June 16-17, 2013 is beyond calculation. As Darchula (Nepal) forms that part of geographical region, the swollen Mahakali river was as devastating as other rivers of Uttarakhand of India.

To single out a few big dam and hydropower projects constructed on the basis of agreements reached between the two countries continue to be controversial. The Koshi dam and the afflux bund constructed for the protection of the barrage did not only threaten the barrage but also inflicted great damage to Nepal. The half of the river entered into the Nepali territory taking lives and property. The cultivable lands were turned into *bagar* (sand). According to the agreement, the government of India is required to protect, maintain and regulate the barrage as well as the dam. Sometimes, lack of adequate precaution taken in advance might cause disaster. It is also true that no one can assume the extent of damage to be caused by the excessive rains resulting in the rise of rivers to such level that is beyond imagination.

Controversy over the use or misuse of rivers both by the upper riparian state like Nepal and the lower riparian state like India has become common in today's Nepal-India relations. And the open border regime existing since time immemorial constitutes a part of such controversy. Yet, in recent years, the reports of over flooding near the dams constructed by India are decreased. The issue of Mahalisagar, Laxmanpur dams, for example, is casually raised during the monsoon because the Indian side has also tried to address it by making provision for the passage of water.

According to a report by Kantipur on July 2013, the Laxmanpur dam has been constructed by blocking the Rapti river at a distance of 300 meter of Nepal-India border pillar no. 19 and meter 650 from the pillar no. 21. It is constructed at a distance of 4.5 kilometre from the border. However, Nepali residing near the border complained that they have been affected by the water-logging problem and inundation. Since the dam (barrage) is of 284 meter long and 5.5 meter high, possibility of flood on the Nepali side is high. Perhaps due to lack of prior knowledge about the possible effects on the other side of the border, it became controversial. However, such problems often arise that need to be tackled immediately. Many joint meetings have taken place to sort out the vexing problem of floods and inundation. Sometimes, the Nepali side has also proposed to return to the pre-construction status but it was decided to send joint teams to conduct on-the spot study and find remedial measures. It was also allegedly agreed that India would not construct such dams near the border without consulting Nepal. Now the dam has already been constructed and made use of it by India, some measures need to be taken to address the flood situation being created by the construction of the dam.

Another dam that has drawn attention of the Nepalis is Mahalisagar dam constructed by India near the border. This dam is 10-km to the south of Taulihawa, district headquarters of Kapilbastu. Constructed by blocking the Mahasai river, it is at a distance of 150 meter from the border. The problem raised by the Nepali side is the same: flooding the Nepali side by the water logged due to the construction of the dam. In fact, the Mahalisagar is not a new dam, as it was constructed by the British in 1901[5].

Khurd, Russiawal and Lotan are three areas where the Bund (*Tat Bund*) is constructed. It is thus named after these three areas. So "it is not the Barrage or Dam. It is about 6 km. from Lumbini, the birth place of Lord Buddha. This bund is a part of 47.5 km long Kanda-Ghoghi bund (K.G. Bund). Here also the problem is centred on water-logging or inundation on the Nepali side. It has been said by the Nepali side that 18 villages are affected by the heavy rainfall resulting in flooding. India has allayed Nepali fears by stating that the bund does not inundate the Nepali territory as it is not a dam. Moreover, as the Indian government maintains, it is regulated by six regulators that prevents from flooding on the Nepali territory[6].

Most of the controversies raised in the context of dam, barrage, afflux bund or bund are not complex and insurmountable. If the two sides agree on addressing such problems and take appropriate timely decisions, they can be easily tackled. However, the issue of upper riparian and lower riparian countries often arise regarding the distribution of waters or for the use of water resources. In the context of Nepal and India, the lower riparian India also raises the issue of excessive floods caused by the rivers flowing from Nepal to India. The Koshi river which was/is called "the sorrow of Bihar" sometimes create havoc causing heavy damage to both lives and property. There are other small and big rivers with potential of inflicting losses to both the countries. Yet, these rivers are also great assets for both the countries. Here also cooperative and coordinated approach of both neighbours can alone help resolve many of such outstanding issues. Instead of blaming each other for causing floods, transparent and positive mind sets on both sides would work to the benefit of both the countries.

5.3 Border Dispute or Encroachment Issue

Border dispute or encroachment issue has been analyzed in the following two different sections.

---

5   See Buddhai Narayan Shrestha, *Nepal Bharat Simawarti Bandh*(Indo-Nepal Frontier Dam) (Kathmandu, VS. 2066),p.133.

6   Ibid, p.166

5.3.1 Claims and Counter Claims

The border dispute between Nepal-India seems to be one of the major factors in damaging Nepal-India relations. In fact, there are allegations and counter-allegations on encroachment by people residing in the border region. Till recently, persons and groups in Nepal have alleged that there are as many as 54 disputed areas with approximately 60,000 hectares encroached by India.[7] But it is said that there are claims and counterclaims at 71 different locations with approximately 60, 662 hectares of land. If one follows Buddhi Narayan Shrestha, surveyor and "expert" on border, out of 26 districts of Nepal which have border link with 21 districts have some sort of border related disputes i.e. issue of encroachment, obstacles, etc[8]. The border was encroached at 53 places 10 years back and it has reached 71 places till today[9]. According to him, Kalapani area (37 thousand hectares of Nepali territory) is the largest area of dispute and half a ropani plot of Pashupatinagar, Ilam is the smallest area. The details of the unresolved spots and pockets of Nepal-India border, according to Shrestha's book 'Sima Sangram (Border War)', is available in annex 3 of this report. Interestingly, media also subscribe his view and as a result the issue has assumed nationalistic tones in Nepal.

Similar feeling is found on Indian side as well. According to an Indian scholar, similar incidences of Nepalese people encroaching upon Indian land in the states of Bihar and Uttar Pradesh have been reported in the Indian media in the past few years[10].The local media in India reports saying that the 6000 hector land in Susta village near India-Nepal border has been captured by Nepal. According to the media report, the land of Susta is neither in Nepal's map nor in India's, but now it has become haven for criminals[11]. According to another media report, Nepali Maoists

---

7 Pushpita Das, "Towards a Regulated India-Nepal border", *Strategic Analysis*, Vol. 32, No. 5, September 2008, p. 883.

8 The Himalayan Talk: Buddhi Narayan Shrestha on Indo-Nepal border, Published on Jul 29, 2012, and available at http://www.youtube.com/watch?v=sTZdUsoSmZY.

9 "India Accused of Encroaching Border at 71 Places", *Republica*, April 5, 2013, also see Weekly Interview of Buddhi Narayan Shrestha, *Republica*, July 18, 2013.

10 Pushpita Das, "Demarcate the India-Nepal Border", IDSA COMMENT, August 31, 2009.

11 See, India-Nepal disputed land becomes haven for criminals, Sahara Samay, April 5, 2013, available at http://www.youtube.com/watch?v=E0126f2F-xQ; Also watch NDTV report on "Disputed Susta a Safe Haven for Criminals", Aug 22, 2009 available at http://www.

entered into the India side of the border, destroyed pillars (Pillar No. 66, 67 and 623) and put their flags in Indian side of the border of Shopthari in Shravasti District[12]. Though Indian authority defines such incident as a minor dispute, Indian media started targeting Indian security arguing that it has failed to secure Indian Territory[13]. Also, Indian security states that Nepal has encroached its border in other places i.e. in Brahmadev in Tanakpur (Uttarakhanda), Shopthari (Uttar Pradesh), and in some parts of Bihar. During our fieldwork, SSB in-charge of Tanakpur BoP stated that Nepalese villagers of Brahmadev area encroached India's territory by hiding/destroying the Border pillar. Once we tried to verify the claim with the locals, some Nepalese accepted the argument saying that "some of the angry Nepalese smashed the border pillar and started claiming some more land after India constructed Tanakpur barrage". But interestingly Buddhi Narayan Shrestha's list also enlists west of Brahmadev Bazar (east of Tanakpur Barrage or area of submerged boundary pillar 2 and 3 and portion of Tanakpur afflux bund) as one of the encroached border by Indian side. In a way, Indian also started arguing and countering the argument about Nepal's claim of border encroachment. And fortunately for Nepalese that issue has not assumed nationalistic tone unlike in Nepal as yet.

While discussing the border encroachment issues, one should not forget the given geographic dynamics in the border region. In other words, major portion of Nepal-India border in such geographical location/condition where "encroachment" becomes more a natural phenomenon than man-made. Rivers flowing from Nepal to India frequently shift their course during the monsoon, transferring some chunks of territory to either Nepal or India. Once there is unused land in the bank of river, local farmers from both countries encroach on this fertile land for cultivation. As Das (2009) writes:

> The main reason for the eruption of such border disputes between India and Nepal is the ever shifting course of the turbulent

---

youtube.com/watch?v=5S9SRJuXRpk.

12 According to a report, Nepali Maoists entered into the India side of the border, destroyed pillars (Pillar No. 66, 67 and 623) and put their flags in Indian Territory. For details, watch http://www.youtube.com/watch?v=i2X0z5krajg.

13 See India TV report broadcasted on 25 May 2009, available at http://www.youtube.com/watch?v=i2X0z5krajg

Himalayan Rivers, which define the international boundary between the two countries in many areas. These rivers keep changing their courses every now and then, thereby throwing up new territories and submerging old land. Although the riverine boundary is determined on the principle of a fixed boundary, the shifting course of rivers results in adverse possessions. In other words, because the river dissolves old lands and creates new ones, the new lands are "illegally" occupied by people beyond the border. So, what was once Nepalese territory is occupied by Indians and vice versa. This process creates confusion and tensions among people residing in these ever changing border landscapes. quote source.

In fact, Das has found the crux of the problem. It is not only Das, there are other researchers, who try to be realistic while discussing Nepal-India border issue. Even Indian journalists seem to have followed some ethnic lines while reporting such a sensitive issue. A report published in *Times of India* from Bahrainch (Uttar Pradesh) reads:

Changing moods of rivers have often caused border dispute between India and Nepal. Every year, several border pillars are either washed away by the flood or get damaged and the two countries have to start all over again the exercise of demarcation which only furthers the dispute. Ghagra and Saryu rivers at Bahraich, Rapti at Shravasti and Sharda at Lakhimpur-Kheri enter the Indian Territory from Nepal. The rivers spread to several kilometers on the Nepal border, several pillars of which stand in the middle of their course. The rivers have run into several other points in the past decade and their course has changed. The pillars which used to be on the other side of the border are now placed across the river. There are many such border pillars which stand in the course of the river and it is a tough job to identify them, thus creating difficulty, making Maoist organisations of Nepal point a finger at India[14].

Shrestha often claims that there are all total 71 cases of encroachment and disturbance, more than a half places have some connection with river course. But if one follows his speeches and interviews, one often finds him emotional like some Indophobia. It does not mean that Nepalese do not know this fact. But what we found is that Nepalese experts, scholars and

---

14 Overflowing rivers wash away Indo-Nepal borderlines, *Times of India*, September 23, 2012.

even media have become emotional while talking about Nepal-India border issue. Even Shrestha has mentioned in many places that 'encroachment' issue of Nepal-Indian border is more a natural phenomenon. Let's take an example of a reporting by Kantipur daily; it has published a report on September 7, 2013 with a title "Purbi Seema Kshetra Atikraman" (Encroachment of Eastern Border) in page 13 of its print version. The report reads:

> According to a recent field study of APF, some 19 pillars are found missing in Pachthar border. Border pillars of 44.38 kilometers area from Sandakpur to Phalaicha are continuously missing. Those which are remaining there are also found in poor condition...Police informed that out of total 113 (23 main, 49 Subsidiary, and 41 small) pillars, only the 94 were found. The report by APF mentions that 20 pillars are due for maintenance, whereas quite a few are at risk due to landslide.

If we read the report carefully, one gets a sense that it has suggested to have a border security post in Nepal's border in Panchthar district. But to draw attention of readers, , media persons tend to lose sight and start sensitizing the issue. . Even the so-called experts fall prey to such sensational propaganda about India-Nepal border situation. Shrestha, for instance, states that the Nepal India Joint Technical Committee formed in 1981 had "settled 97 per cent of border demarcation disputes and prepared 182 strip maps. Surveyors from both Nepal and India have put their signatures on those maps. Only three per cent work remains, including on disputed regions of Susta and Kalapani[15]". In the same interview, he states that "there are claims and counterclaims at 71 different locations, and altogether 60, 662 hectares of land are under encroachment and cross-holding"[16].

Having said that it should be concluded that the issues raised by a section of the people in Nepal are not as problematic as they have tried to project it. Nor are they deliberately created by the Indian side. They simply seem to be local problems deserving immediate local level settlement. As Nihar writes, Maoist Chairperson Pushpa Kamal Dahal, during a visit to India, acknowledged the problem of inundation in the border areas and

---

15 see his interview published in *Republica*, http://www.myrepublica.com/portal/index.php?action=news_details&news_id=57978

16 ibid.

agreed to take up necessary work for its effective prevention on the basis of bilateral consultation. However, the issue of border encroachment rose to prominence again after Dahal's resignation from the post of Prime Minister in 2009. His party has accused Indian security forces of encroaching Nepalese territory in many places including Dang district. In fact, it was the Maoist Party which mobilized different teams led by senior leaders to different border disputed areas during the year of 2009/2010. Dahal who was to attend such protest programme in Kalapani of Darchula District cancelled the program at the last movement. However, he couldn't resist blaming India for border encroachment. Addressing a mass meeting in Dang he argued for 'Greater Nepal' saying that the relevance of Sugauli Treaty has been ended and Nepal need to claim its land from Teesta in the East and Kangada in the West. "The treaty was signed not with India and Indian people, but with Angrej (the British). Along with the end of British, the relevance of the treaty has also been over," Dahal states[17].

Also Kathmandu based media is often found in creating havoc about the border dispute. Take the example of January 30, 2009, and June 1, 2009. Some sections of the Nepalese media claimed that the Shashastra Seema Bal (SSB) had encroached upon Nepalese land and constructed camps. News reports claimed that around 1800 Nepali villagers were driven out of around 22 border villages in Dang district by the SSB. Subsequent reports picked up the number of displaced villagers from 'Dang-Kapilvastu border area to Dang-Banke point' as more than 6000. Quoting local sources, the news reports also alleged that Darjeeling forest officials had also tried to build infrastructure in Nepal's Ilam district. However, India strongly denied these news reports and claimed that they were false and fabricated allegations by certain people aimed at disturbing friendly relations between India and Nepal. The Indian embassy in Kathmandu also issued a statement asserting that it has cross-checked the facts from Indian and Nepalese district authorities and they had clarified that no such violation of the international border had taken place. Not only the local government officials (Chief District Officer) but also the District Police officer denied the report published by the media.

Supporting all these stands, Foreign Minister of Nepal Sujata Koirala also dismissed reports of Indian encroachment in Dang and Bara districts and stated that the investigation team sent by the Nepalese government did

---

17 Sudheer Sharma, *Prayogshala*, Kathmandu: Fine Print. 2013. pp.309-310.

not come across any such incidents. But the media reaction was interesting (*herna layak*) which tried its best to ridicule Ms. Koirala without any base[18]. Once it was not accepted by media, a team of eighteen parliamentary parties of the Constituent Assembly headed by legislator Amik Sherchen inspected 22 border points from Bara to Dang to investigate the allegations. A second team comprising members of the Foreign Relations and Human Rights Committee of parliamentarians headed by lawmaker Padma Lal Bishwakarma visited the 'affected' areas. Why? Is it due to trust deficit of government body? Or is it due to political leaders' will to go with popular sentiment. The similar case seems to be dominant always while discussing Nepal-India relations, border, etc. The government officials of Nepal and India say that a joint team from both countries has already surveyed and found three areas where the two countries disagreed on the border – Pashupati Nagar in the east, Susta in the south and Kalapani in the west of Nepal[19]. But media continues to believe in some individuals who harp on 71 encroachments spots.

5.3.2 Facts and Figures

Our research also realized that there are a couple of areas on dispute in Nepal-India border. Being two different nation-states, Nepal and India have to maintain their border, and for that, a clear and well-maintained Noman's land is important. Our team has observed that the places like Pashupatinagar in Ilam, Jogbani in Morang, Alau and Inarwa (Janaki Tole in Nepali side) in Parsa, Balara (Basvitta in Indian side)[20] and Arnah (Sujawa in Indian side) in Sarlahi where there is no clear and maintained no-man's land (*Das Gaja*). It was surprising that both the Indian Custom and Immigration offices in Pashupatinagar border are either in the Noman's land or in Nepal's territory. Just behind the offices, there are a couple of personal houses which were constructed in the middle of *Dasgaja* area. Interestingly, there is a house with two gates; one is on Indian side and another on Nepal side. If somebody inters into the house from one country, he can be in another country just by using another door of the house. Similar situation was found in Jogbani gate of Nepal-India border.

---

18 For details see http://www.youtube.com/watch?v=9hMGMd2QOqw.

19 Gyanu Adhikari, "Nepal-India agree to find missing border pillars, enhance security", *The Hindu*, June 3, 2013.

20 See Figure 2 to see how pillars are encroached by locals

(Pictures showing pillars being encroached by locals in Balara-Basvitta area)

There is no open space but full of fruit stalls and huts between Nepal and Indian Custom offices. If somebody wants to cross the border, he/she can do it in Jogbani without coming to the street. Likewise, a gravel road which is 8-feet wide becomes divider of Nepal-India border in Alau Village in Parsa, and Raxaul whereas hardly 3 feet wide space in available in dividing two countries in Inarwa-Janaki Tole point of Nepal-India border. For the villagers, border pillar seems isignificant as it is lying on someone's yard or in the middle of the gravel road. More so, Indian citizens are using no man's land in Balara-Basvitta area[21] (see the above photographs), and Nepalese are using the border land in Arnah-Sujawain[22] area (see the photograph below). But these facts have not been made big issues in Kathmandu and in Delhi. It may be due to the fact that there is no fight between the citizens of two countries residing along these borders.

Picture showing border pillar being encroached by locals in Arnah-Sujawain

The existing situation of Junge pillar PP- 1 of Bhadrapur, Jhapa, is another issue of Nepal-India border which needs proper attention of both the countries. While one crosses Mechi River from Bhadrapur, Jhapa, and

---

21 Middle Pillar number 339/12, small pillar 339/13, 339/14 and 339/15 in this area can be seen nearby tap, buffalo yard, and *Malkhaldo*.

22 Pillar no 337/14 in this area is seen in the middle of vegetable form cultivated by a Yadav of Nepal.

moves towards the way to Galgalia railway station (Bihar), he/she can see a border pillar just after the bank of the river. It is now within the compound of Sashastra Seema Bal, Galgaliya BOP. According to locals, it is one of the Masonry (Junge) Pillar PP-1 of Mechi River constructed on the boundary line between Nepal and India in order to see it as the Tri-junction of Bihar-West Bengal-Nepal Border. But once Mechi River changed its course towards Nepali side, the pillar was seen situated towards Indian side. Then, India has usaed it to make hut for SSB attaching it to Junge pillar ignoring the area of No-man's Land. Such cases can be noticed in many other places but it seems to be a particular case that gives two facts:

> While talking about border encroachment issue, generally it is locals who are involved in illegal occupation of river created new land in bordering areas. But this particular case is made a state created issue.

> The pillar is visible to everybody, neither is it damaged nor washed away by the river.

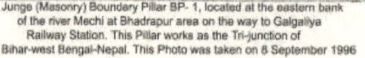

Junge (Masonry) Boundary Pillar BP- 1, located at the eastern bank of the river Mechi at Bhadrapur area on the way to Galgaliya Railway Station. This Pillar works as the Tri-junction of Bihar-west Bengal-Nepal. This Photo was taken on 6 September 1996

Photograph of the Masonry (Junge) Pillar PP-1 of Mechi River which is now under SSB Camp cited by Buddhi Narayan Shrestha.

Maintaining Nepal border up to the border pillar by going beyond the Mechi River might have been a difficult task. But those who were involved in addressing border issue had to go for transparent solution, one of which might be the commensurate compensation of land to Nepal. Instead of thinking of the complication and complexity of such issue, it is said that the field level Nepal-India joint border survey team regarded the Junge as the reference pillar (RP) while they were working on the Mechi river sector during December 1995. That is why it has become difficult to believe for the people who were eye witness throughout the changes. During our field visit, SSB was telling that it is one of the RPs but not the Junge Pillar but to which no locals were prepared to accept such statement.

On the top of all, Kalapani in the Far West and Susta in Nawalparasi have been always in lime light in Nepal-India border relations. Kalapani is the most disputed area of Nepal-India border which lies in Kalapani-Lilmpiadhura area of Darchula district. According to Nepal, after the India-China war in 1962, Nepal allowed Indian troops to occupy some posts in Nepal as a defensive measure. India has withdrawn from all of them, except Kalapani. It apparently wants to hold on to that post[23]. In other words, there is a history behind the dispute of 37,000 hectares of land there. It is said that during the 1962 Indo-China war, Indians were looking for a place where they could be safe in order to halt the Chinese troops were the latter to make further inroads into India. Indian troops found Kalapani the perfect place to do so. They thought they could use the 20,276-feet high altitude area for effective defence against the Chinese. Since 1962, the Indian troops have stationed in Kalapani, and "China recognised it as land of India[24]".

However, bilateral talks have often taken place about the settlement of border issues including Kalapani. During Prime Minister G.P. Koirala's visit to India in July-August 2000, there was a convergence of views

---

23   Alok Kumar Gupta , Kalapani: A Bone of Contention Between India and Nepal, IPCS Comment, 17 October 2000, available at http://www.ipcs.org/article/nepal/kalapani-a-bone-of-contention-between-india-and-nepal-422.html

24   According to Maniraj Upadhyay (former editor of Samaj), King Mahendra accepted India's request not only to construct a Check Post but also to station its security force. Once Rishikesh Shaha asked the late King Mahendra about Kalapani . The King, who wanted not to annoy India any longer,, told Shaha that it was not the issue under his Ministry. For details, *Yesari Gumyo Kalapani* (This is how Kalapani was lost), *Nepal National Weekly*, Vol. 14, No 10, October 6, 2013.

between Mr. Koirala and Prime Minister Atal Bihari Vajpayee on matters of far reaching importance relating to political, security and development co-operation. It has been agreed that field-work for the demarcation of the boundary will be completed by AD 2001-2002 and final strip maps will be prepared by 2003. Significantly, the Joint Boundary Committee also agreed that in case both sides were unable to reach a mutually acceptable agreement on specific segments (referring to two pockets on the boundary- Kalapani in the West and West Champaran in the South, which have defied resolution), detailed reports including a compilation of available evidence would be submitted to the two governments for consideration. It is said that the External Affairs Ministry in India, however, has rigidly opposed the withdrawal of troops from Kalapani and maintains that the issue has been exaggerated. According to New Delhi, "such a withdrawal will have adverse bearing on India's security[25]."

Regarding Susta in Nawalparasi, it has been considered as the second largest disputed area with 14,500 Hectares of land. Like other disputed parts of Nepal-India border, nature seems to have played a big role in Susta border controversy too. By the time Nepal signed Sugauli Treaty on March 4, 1816, it was said that Narayani River was flowing towards north-south from Tribeni Ghat of Nawalparasi. Subsequent floods changed the river course and started eroding Nepali side thus compelling many Nepalese to find a new settlement. It is said that Narayani river changes its course towards the west (*that means towards Nepal side*) along with floods; it has changed its course by cutting some 12800 hectors of Nepali land in 1902 (B.S.). Likewise some 6000 hectors of Nepali land were cut by the flood in 2011 (B.S.), more 1000 hectors in 2019 (B.S.), and finally 150 hectors in 2037 (B.S.)[26].That is how the whole Susta, which was earlier one of the Village Panchayats of Nawalparasi district, became bank of river. The settlers of the Panchayat were displaced. Many of them having valid documents such as citizenship and land ownership certificates were rehabilitated in different areas of Tribeni Panchayat but those who had no evidences were left out. That is how Susta VDC was merged into Tribeni VDC in 2034 (B.S.). But the story of Susta continued taking different colours. Slowly, those who were left out in getting land due to lack of citizenship had a difficult time to face. Since Nepal government did nothing to address their problem, some

---

25 ibid

26 Roshan Kumar Jha, *Seema Samashya Ma Rajniti* (Politics in Border Problem), *Nayapatrika*, Baisakh 18, 2070.

of them started going back to Susta and resumed farming in the empty land. Also, those who were staying in bordering areas of both Nepal and India, and were in search of fertile land also joined the flood victims to occupy the empty land. They started gathering support by inviting their relatives, friends etc[27]. Since it was very fertile land, it could attract crowd easily. Once it became a small village of majority of people of Nepali origin, the Nepali state tried to own this territory by putting the area under ward no 4 of the Triveni VDC of Nawalparasi district.

Our research team visited Susta area to understand the disputed area objectively. It is found that land being used by the Nepalese now has no ownership and registration certificate. Locals including Gopal Gurung state that the land they are using today was a grazing field before the flood washed away the Susta village. According to Jha, people don't have land ownership certificate of those lands, and the cause behind it was the politics of the then government. "In the name of resolving the disputes, the land which were under the ownership of Madhesi people were distributed to Ex-army families in 2022 (B.S.) by Royal government. That is why no one has ownership Certificates of those land", he writes[28] While discussing about the land with the locals in Susta, we sensed that the problem has arisen not due to other reason but due to the fertile nature of the land. "Since it is very fertile land, many of them hold this land to make good earning. The people used this land as a transit. Once they have money, they either settle in Indian side or in Nepal," a police officer in Susta states. The "total 21980 hector lands were owned by the Susta Panchayat before. We occupy almost 7000 hectors of land today without any legal registration", Gurung says. According to him, he, who served the Nepal Government as police personnel till 1995, started living in Susta area from 1996. Before that he used to visit this area for the purpose of hunting. "I had developed good friendship with people like Tek Narayan Upadhyay of Susta Panchayat, and I used to visit this area through this connection. Eventually, I shifted to Susta from Tanahu district as I started liking the environment and fertile nature of land of Susta. The life was very easy during those days but afterwards, people started facing difficulties in Sushta", Gopal Gurung states[29].

---

27 Based on the group discussion with Gopal Gurung and other locals of Susta Save Movement, Susta

28 Roshan Kumar Jha, *Seema Samashya Ma Rajniti* (Politics in Border Problem), *Nayapatrika*, Baisakh 18, 2070.

29 Researcher's interview with Gurung (September 9, 2013 at 9.30 and 10.03 am)

The Susta village has now 225 households with 3,133 population. Till recently there were 337 houses but 112 households were chased away towards Indian side. The reason behind this punishment is that they supported India, and "supplied information" of Save Susta Movement to Indian Agencies. Those who were chased away from the village still have their land in the Susta area but they shifted their house to Indian side of the border due to the perceived insecurity. According to Gopal Gurung, there are still some 43 to 50 Indian families residing in Susta area[30].

We could see a chunk of unused land in Susta village, facing the Gandak Baraj to the north. It is said that the unused land is about 14,000 hectors. According to locals it was the actual land of Susta Panchayat before it was washed away by the Narayani (Gandak) river. Due to its very fertile nature, both the Indian and Nepalese locals wanted to occupy the land. But the issue is often made sensational by raising nationalistic sentiments by the help of media if there is some encroachment by locals. That is why the border security forces of both Nepal and India agreed not to allow anybody to use the unused land. "It is very fertile land; a farmer gets at least 100 thousand a year if he/she cultivates sugarcane in a hector of land. That is why there is a tough fight among the locals to occupy unused land. Even if it is fight of locals to occupy more land in order to earn more, the issue is carried to media dragging it into controversy. If somebody ploughs one Kattha of land, others claim that there was encroachment of 10 hector", Inspector of APF, Susta Mr. Siyaram Chaudhary states[31].

In fact, we find no border pillar around. Also there is no SSB post as in other points of the border. However they have a BOP some kilometres away. It seems that they have decided to stay slightly away from the controversial area to avoid possible conflict with the locals. Yet, there are Nepal Police Post, a school and a Security Base of APF, Nepal. Locals (Nepalese) also acknowledged that the land which they have claimed today as being part of Nepal was an unused or public land (grazing land) before. They say that the land of Susta Panchayat was vanished not due to man-made cause but due to unpredicted natural factor as it was washed away by Narayani River while changing its course. Even the chairperson of Save Susta Movement, Gurung, does not forget to acknowledge present Susta as new land. In his view, most of the residents of this area are also new as they were invited

---

30 Researcher's interview with Gurung (September 9, 2013 at 9.30 and 10.03 am)
31 Researcher's interview with Chaudhary (May 10, 2013)

recently once some of the displaced families explored the fertile land here. Once we observed the situation in the field, we came to a conclusion that the issue is not as complicated as media and so-called border experts projected.

While going into the details in order to find the crux of the problem, what we sensed was that both Nepal and India became hostage of the so-called locals of Susta. Those who are earning quite a good amount of money by using the controversial land, pay land tax neither to Nepal nor to India. It is said that Munna Khan alone, who lives in Paklihawa village of Nawalparasi, has about 200 hectors land in Susta area. They get political mileage by raising their voices as if they are fighting to save the soil of their motherland. It is heard that some of the leading figures have already bagged some awards by Nepali state for their "extraordinary jobs". Also scholars, experts and media often quote them as if they are the authorities of the area. However, as stated by police officer earlier, most of them are there in the transit earning sufficient money by using the most fertile land without paying tax. It seems that they take extreme position to support/oppose either India or Nepal to avoid certain personal risks. . It is also found that many of them have criminal cases, and have taken shelter in another country to avoid punishment. For example, there are people i.e. Lalina Begum, Adam Khan, Gopal Gurung named by many Nepali scholars, media and experts as Nepal's border guards. But if one knows their personal profile, he/she will be hesitant to quote them. As mentioned earlier, Gurung is not the native but a newcomer in the area which he himself acknowledged. All three are found in India's most wanted criminal lists. More interestingly, Lalina Begum was one who simultaneously holds citizenship of both the countries and takes state privileges accordingly. In an interview[32], she herself acknowledged that she is having citizenship of both the countries[33]. Knowing these details, a couple of questions often come to our mind. They are:

> What is the logic behind the state support to those people, who hold double citizenship, pay no taxes to the state authority, and become instrumental to damage two neighbor's relations?

---

32 http://www.youtube.com/watch?v=E0126f2F-xQ.

33 While we tried to verify it, Gopal Gurung argues saying that she is Nepali citizen, and all her family members are having Nepali citizenship. He further states that she has taken Indian citizenship in order to go to Haz, and she had to do so after she was denied citizenship by Nepal (as per discussion with Gurung, September 9, 2013.

> What is the logic for a state's presence there (to keep police post and APF) if the state cannot ensure property rights of the locals. In other words, if Nepali state has evidence or proof of its territory, it has to issue land ownership certificate, tax the farmers as per rule, and provide all sorts of security including rights to property.

Unfortunately, the Nepali state has forgotten both the points mentioned above while being a part of Susta controversy. In a way, it has not undergone a detailed study as it seems to work under political pressure. It is high time for Nepal to act on the basis of a thorough study. The following points seem to have impacted the government action in the past:

> Nepal-India border was one of the neglected issues of both the countries till recently.

> No independent research was conducted.

> In absence of an in-depth research, a few activists and others monopolize the agenda making politicians hesitant to make decision on the issue.

> If one has monopoly in interpreting data, he/she wants to take a more populist line. Thus, facts are diluted in the garb of nationalistic position. Such campaigns have served some political parties to score their objective of being nationalist. But, it has hardly helped settle the vexing problem of border.

Instead of settling these controversies by understanding the field reality, political leaders go out of track and support these movements. Once they were ousted from power in 2009, Maoist leaders visited key points of the Nepal-India border as part of their campaign for 'national independence'. At the disputed Susta, Baburam Bhattari said that Nepalis had to fight against foreign intervention and internal reactionary forces together. He said his party had taken on the expansionists who encroached border with the help of internal reactionary elements, comprador and bourgeoisie and feudalism. Visiting Pashupatinagar border, the then Vice President of the UCPN-Maoist Mohan Baidya warned, "We want to move ahead together with India and China for progress and development. But we are ready to fight if the Indian authorities put up unnecessary hurdles." Meanwhile, at Mahendranagar, Pushpa Kamal Dahal stated: "Let this not be misunderstood as a ploy to sour Nepal-India relations. It is not that we want to fight with foreigners and capture their land, but we will not tolerate if someone eyes our nation." Though the statements were nothing more than abstractions, it seems that such mobilization of parties has always encouraged those unscrupulous elements residing near the border.

Nevertheless, such a situation does not wholly exist today. Along with the deployment of SSB in Indian side and APF *Seema Surakshya Karyalaya* in Nepali side, both the governments have not only tried to understand the different dynamics of open border but have also given attention to the border. And it has been an attempt to break knowledge hegemony of a few who claim to be experts on Nepal-India border. Wherever we met security officials of both the countries' border guard force, we found them quite confident in discussing different aspects of Nepal- India border. "We have now made a proper record of our border points. That is why, no more encroachment or dispute is possible in the future", almost all the officers of APF Seema Surakshya Karyalaya deployed in the bordering area say. The map on the opposite page substantiates the aforementioned argument.

Acknowledgement and understanding of most of the APF officers who belong to hill communities in Nepal seem to be very interesting and that should be taken as one of the positive notes to avoid unnecessary controversy and exaggeration related to Nepal-India border issue. Those who were fed by anti-India sentiments in the past have now realized that the border is not as complicated as media reported. Neither the encroachment nor issues under dispute are serious. Many high ranking APF officers interviewed states: "Issue of border encroachment in Nepal-India border is either false or over exaggerated by the media. Before going into details of how the situation is being changed towards positive direction, politicians and media people seem to highlight negative aspects more than the positive changes taking place over the years.

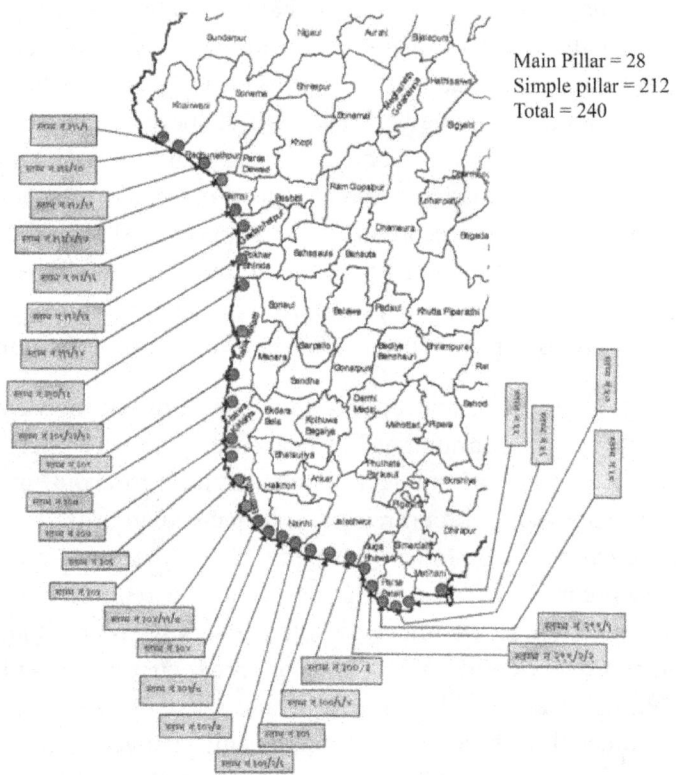

(Map marking of main pillars in the border area of Mahottari, Source: Mahottari APF

Source: Pradip Raj Kanel, Nepal-India Border Management: A Study Related to Bordering Mahottari District, An unpublished research, 2012

Chapter VI : Causes Behind The Border Related Problems: An Analysis

Talking about the issue of smuggling, border dispute or any other kinds of border related issues, it has been quite often observed that there is trust deficit between the security apparatuses of two countries. The major complain comes from Nepali side regarding drug and betel nut (supari). They often state that they could not secure help of Indian security on controlling drug , betel nut. Indian security seems to be more concerned about smuggling of Hasish, Charesh, Fake Currency, and about those who are listed as Criminals in India. Lack of coordination of the security apparatus deployed in the border can be observed in some of the bordering points. Lack of trust was / is observed in the eastern borders, but controlling criminals along with drugs and hashish all over the border seems to create problem. Why it happens? Some of its answers are as follows:

Superiority-inferiority complex: Despite being a very positive attitude of Indian security personnel especially the SSB deployed in bordering areas during our fieldwork, some of the Nepali officers complain about 'big brothers' attitude of Indian side. Similarly the Indian personnel complain that some Nepalese officers do not want to be frank enough with Indian officials. It seems that both the hill mindset of Nepal along with the inferiority complex is somehow working. Such a situation was found even at the people's level. "There is always a dominating attitude of Indian officials toward Nepalese," some of the social activists working in bordering areas state while we were having an interaction on border issue on September 15, 2013. But interestingly, both the sides have acknowledged that they can do much if there was coordination between two security apparatuses deployed in the bordering areas. "There was border dispute in Bardiya, near Gularia. Nepalese locals had a long list of complaints against the SSB, for encroaching agriculture land. But,neither the APF nor other agencies had approached the SSB before as we had a feeling that they won't listen. But once I came here, I called on the counterpart (SSB official) and discussed about it. Once they knew the grievances, we went through the documents that the local possessed, and accordingly decided to withdraw from that particular land," SSP of APF of Bardiya says. While we were doing fieldwork, we saw an example of trust deficit and lack of coordination. Here is an example of such an incident. While we were discussing with CDO of Rupandehi, the latter received a phone call by his intelligence officer. It was related to locals' complain about border encroachment by the SSB while it was constructing its BoP. Once the CDO knew it, he called up all the security agencies of the district including Survey officer (Naapi) and suggested to go together to observe the situation. Then, all together 7 district level officers including CDO, SP and SSP of Rupandehi police, DSP of APF, In-charge of Intelligence Agency, In-charge of *Naapi* office went to the area which was some 20 kilometres away from the district headquarters. As it was a border related issue, we also followed them. Once we were there, an awkward situation developed. Construction work of BoP (India) was going on and was being supervised by a Hawaldar of SSB. Seeing all high ranking Nepalese officials, he was surprised but didn't lose his confidence. He asked us if there was any urgency. "Is there any urgent matter to discuss sir? Shall I call my officer sir?" But Nepalese officers said that they were there to observe the situation as they received a complaint about the border encroachment. Then, Nepalese team asked for a tape to measure the no man's land. Fortunately, it was the area where no-man's land was properly managed. We could observe that there was more than enough space for Dasgaja or No Man's Land between the point of construction and Nepal border. Embarrassed as they were, the Nepli team members returned without uttering a word about the so-called encroachment.

This incident should be analyzed positively and negatively as well. It is positive because Nepal has shown sensitivity towards its border. However, one also needs to analyze seriously before visiting the site. Though it was the highest level team of the district level led by the CDO, the team went there in vain without having any document i.e. the map etc. Neither was there any presence of locals so that they could tell the situation. Also, since it was the matter of two countries, it would have been better to inform the Indian counterparts before going there. In a way, it was waste of time and resources in the name of sensitivity of the border. It would have been better if CDO would have sent one of the officers to report the fact based on the observation. Similar case was explained by Kanchanpur SP of APF. But

Causes Behind The Border Related Problems: An Analysis

the CDO and the SP handled the case differently. According to SP, people from Dodhara/Chandani areas of Kanchanpur filed a complaint saying that Indian locals have encroached no man's land in the area. Once it was informed, they decided to send a DSP of APF to report the details. DSP went there and met his counterparts in order to discuss the matter. SSB and DSP of APF together came to a controversial site, measured the noman's land. "We were ashamed after we found that Indian had left the necessary area unused for the purpose of no man's land. Unfortunately, it was Nepal side of no man's land which was not left unused for the purpose but was used by local Nepalese for their agriculture purpose", says the DSP. Also, there was another example of coordination that we have observed during our fieldwork. Let us take an example of Hotel Kosi, Kakarbhitta. At around 9.00 PM, a West Bengal police jeep came towards Kakarbhitta with Nepali police. The jeep stopped in front of Hotel Kosi. All the passengers of the jeep came out and moved towards the Hotel. They roamed around, talk to both hotel people and locals outside the Hotel. One officer was speaking to his junior (Nepal police officer) saying that the Indian counterpart (West Bengal Police) needed help as directed by CDO, Jhapa. That meant they have already talked to CDO. Before going back to Fulbari, the West Bengal police officers thanked Nepali counterparts for their help.

Again the next morning at around 7.00, a vehicle with 3 dressed up security personnel along with 3-4 civilians crossed the Mechi Bridge and came toward Nepal side. The vehicle was stopped in front of Nepal police office, and spent 5-7 minute there. Then, the vehicle came to Kakarbhiitta Bazaar and stopped again in front of Hotel Kosi. Three security personnel started investigation. No Nepali counterpart was there at that time. Afterwards the vehicle went back to Fulbari, but some policemen remained there. Their activity was related to a story of a cab stolen from India. Initially it was hired in India and the driver was given a position in a hotel and the cab was taken to Nepal. They came to Kakarbhiitta, booked Kosi Hotel, enjoyed meal and stayed there for two nights. They requested the hotel that they would pay the bill later after coming back from Ilam. Once the hotelier insisted them to pay, the thief deposited the key of the cab and left the cab in Hotel's parking space. But the team never came back to take the cab. Then, the West Bengal police was informed about the cab left by an unknown group. It was known that a complaint was filed by its owner to investigate. That is how the West Bengal Police was in Kakarbhiitta. This is an example of cooperation and coordination at the local level. And this is how the effective border management has been possible given the will and dedication of concerned authorities.

Corruption is another issue that weakens border management. Our team often hears local grievances against the security of both the countries deployed along the border. Both the peoples of India and Nepal state that they could not see proper implementation of security policies due to security agencies' own involvement in corruption. We have observed that SSB and APF introduced similar mechanism i.e. often transfer the security personnel from border points in order to avoid familiarity/rapport with the locals. But, still, majority of locals residing in border area state that the border management agencies including SSB and APF are involved in corruption. "All security apparatus deployed in the bordering areas of both the countries are corrupt...Even the SSB personnel, who are in duty in major border points like Rupaedia, Banbasa, Gaurifanta, cannot take bribes from commoners, but those SSB personnel, who are posted in different places for patrolling the bordering areas collect huge amount of money through "bribes".[1]

Peoples of bordering areas also blame the APF and SSB for supporting to carry out illegal activities. "Nepal police take bribe and allow us to bring household goods without any hurdle. But SSB started controlling us from the Indian side. They allow only 15-20 KG sugar and 5-7 litres of oil/ghee for social functions such as Death Anniversary while the actual need for performing rituals would be much higher. They ask for Rupees 4,000 as bribe for carrying the goods in sufficient quantity". Bindeshwar Yadav, Dinesh Yadav and Shambhu Shah of Kacharwa-7, Bara, told this story with a research team in one of the group discussions[2]. Bribe taking culture of the security and other border agencies seems to be one of the major reasons behind the public grievances against these two institutions. Many local complain against these agencies saying that they often get harassed; their activities were being controlled, etc. Also, even if it is the coincidence, a couple of border regulations were introduced along with the deployment of the SSB and APF in Nepal-India border. For example, the Jamunaha transit point in Nepalganj-Rupaidia, which used to be opened 24 hours

---

[1] Based on researchers' discussion with Netra Panthi, Jhalak Gaire, Gopal Nath Yogi, etc. on December 30, 2012 and September 16, 2013. See also *Kantipur daily*, September 14, 2013.

[2] Research team's discussion with the locals, April 21, 2013.

till recently, now opens only during 4 am to 9 pm. Travellers from across the border who arrive after 9 pm get stranded in the border due to the new regulation. Also, open border was transformed into regulated system in one of the land-routes at Nepalganj-Rupaidiya border crossing point from November 1, 2005. Both the governments introduced regulated border management system to this point, as ID card system had been made compulsory. But it has not been materialized not only due to slackness in border administration, but also due to criticism made by the Nepalese and outsiders saying that the new provision was against the spirit of the 1950 treaty.[3]

However, even if there are many reasons blaming others, it is a major challenge before all, especially the SSB and APF, to prove their integrity. If many locals say that they have paid some amount of bribes to either of the forces, others believe in it. At Birganj Nepal Police caught a truck carrying goods without paying adequate custom duties but was allowed by APF after taking bribe. When people find such cases, they have to believe in similar stories as well. Here, it is interesting to quote Bal Bahadur Khatri, Hotelier in border area. He states:

> Indian Custom police are much corrupt. One sees a kind of drama in the morning when the first bus arrives here from Delhi or from other cities. They are looted by Rikshaw pullers and police, and SSB would provide security to these corrupt agencies. Nepalese would have protested or beaten the Custom Police much before their manhandling behaviour, but they are secured as they are guarded by SSB. Here SSB's presence has been like frontier forces with weapons to safeguard the Corrupt officers. That is why I see SSB's involvement in corruption and loot even if they are not talking money from us directly. I sense that they have built a nexus between other corrupt agencies so that they share benefit out of loot. Otherwise, how can they safeguard those corrupt and looters? We think that we are helpless for being cheated due to SSB.

We have also witnessed a unique way of indulging in corruption by Indian Custom during our fieldwork in Darchula/Dharchula border. They have established a trend there where the shopkeepers of Indian side of the border have to issue a piece of paper with the details of goods one client

---

3 http://nepallaw.blogspot.com/2005/11/question-made-by-border-regulations.html

has bought from his/her shop. The client would collect the paper from the shopkeepers and submit them to the Custom office in the border before he/she crosses border for entering into Nepal. The Custom men would take the commission from the shopkeepers every evening based on the chit collected from the clients. And the shopkeepers would take some extra money from the clients so that they pay it back to the custom office in the evening. "If we request them to pay Custom duty against the goods they carry from Indian side, they often get irritated and argue that how many times we need to pay Customs. For them, the extra amount they have paid while buying goods in India is Custom. That is how we are suffering," Custom officer of Darchula (Nepal) shared it with us.

- Priorities of different security apparatus have been identified as another important cause which helped to produce an inefficient border management.. Though both the security agencies especially APF and SSB were given similar kind of responsibilities, what we have observed is that they often change their priority, and while doing so they won't discuss or take consent of their counterpart of the other side of the border. As a result, one is compelled to see inefficiency in the border. While we were in the field, Nepali side of the security agencies (Nepal Police and APF) were found restless in controlling betelnut smuggling from Nepal to India. We could observe that they were in fact trying hard not to let somebody to stop smuggling, the movement of contraband /illegal goods, import or export without clearing custom duties. The APF has the following broad duties:

- Peace keeping, internal security and prevention of criminals from passing the border

- Security of custom check points, border areas and border pillars, and and prevention of trans-border crimes

- Prevention of girls trafficking

- Prevention of transaction of arms and amenities

- Prevention of transaction of fake currencies, smuggling of betel nut (suparti) towards India.

CAUSES BEHIND THE BORDER RELATED PROBLEMS: AN ANALYSIS

But Smuggled betelnut (*supari*) was easily found nearby border closer to India. It was due to the fact that Indian security, in comparison to Nepal's APF and Police, was not that much concerned about the issue. Once we heard similar complaint by one of the APF Officers in Kakarbhitta, we spent some days in Mechi Bridge to verify the fact. It was in fact interesting to observe it. Though it was very tight in Nepali side, we could see people in the middle of the Mechi Bridge collecting betelnut and supplying it to India. Indian security was not much bothered about it. Some smugglers were there with money to collect betelnut smuggled from Nepal. In doing so, women were used and wore Kurta - Salwar for hiding 1-2 Kg betelnut inside their Salwar. "Since we lack sufficient strength to control the entire border, we have to take SSB's help. But their stand on betelnut is flexible, whereas we get order directly from Home Minister", one Nepal Police officer stated. Asked about it to Indian SSB and State Police, they would reply in abstract saying that we have not allowed any kind of smugglings including betelnut. But their body language was not convincing and the reality in the field also revealed that it was not their priority.

It was quite interesting and difficult to understand why Indian security was flexible to betelnut smugglers as it was India that made a request to Nepal to stop betelnut smuggling. There seems to be two possible causes: (1) Nepal police and APF took it seriously due to the direct order of Nepal's Home Minister who took it seriously as he was requested from Delhi to stop it. The Nepali side seemed to become efficient due to less communication channel that order had to pass through; (2) Indian Police didn't put it in priority as they are yet to receive that particular circulation due to multiplicity of channels. The division of functions between the state and central government might have caused delay in communication with the local custom posts.

Policy Difference

Different policies to deal with certain issues are yet another big problems faced by the border personnel. Both the security forces blame their counterparts for their non-cooperation to combat some illegal cases. Nepalese complain against the sale of some drugs that are not allowed in Nepal. Drug addicts in Nepal have often used these drugs when they do not get the real one. India complains against Nepal for not controlling alcohol drinking activities in Nepali side. But it is only a blame game indulged in by both sides.

Contradictory Government Policies

It was quite visible in Eastern parts of Nepal-India borders in the case of betelnut import and export. The contradiction was between two ministries of Nepal-Home, and commerce and Supply. On the one hand, Ministry of Home was restless to control the smuggling of betelnut, while the Ministry of Commerce and Supply was easily providing import permission to it. All including police officials and businessmen express their displeasure about the unclear contradictory policies of the government. "Everybody knows that there is not much use of betelnut in Nepal. It has been imported to Nepal in a big amount for not Nepal's consumption but to export to India. But what is happening now is that we are allowed to import it legally from 3rd countries, but its movement has been stopped by the police once it enters into Nepal's territory. Businessmen in Kakarbhitta say that "it is ridiculous policy of the government agencies". "How can it be illegal to carry inside the territory of Nepal if it has been imported with due process?" Chairperson of Mechi Udyog Sangh states. "Supari [betelnut] farming is popular in Nepal and but its market is India. In the past, there was legal way to import betelnut from Nepal but after the Nepal government banned it, then the smuggling business flourished[4]. And different means were being used, Lekhanath Dahal, Custom Agent Association, Jogbani. Avinash Bohra of Morang Byapar Sangh also acknowledges that trading of Supari has been facing different challenges. In Jhapa, there is huge farming of betelnut which is not used in Nepal. Nepalese government should be clear its trading policy. Nepal government had restricted the free movement of betelnut in Nepal leading to restriction of its export to India, where levy is heavy on betelnut[5].

Duplication and Lack of clarity

Unclear assignment or duplication of responsibility to more than an organisation has been yet another problem in the bordering areas. Though it was not a big issue in Indian side, it has been quite visible in Nepali side between Nepal Police and Armed Police Force which quite often create problem in border management. APF officers often denied accept

---

4 Discussion with researchers on March 13, 2013.
5 As per discussion with researchers on March 14, 2013.

Causes Behind The Border Related Problems: An Analysis

duplication of the duty saying that border management has been assigned only to APF. Nepal Police officers while talking to the research team often stated that it is one of the major problems. A few incidents have proved that their relationship is not as satisfactory as they pretend to show. The incident of August 2, 2013, in which teams of Nepal Police and Armed Police Force (APF) clashed in Birganj over a loaded truck, can be taken as an example. Based on a tip off that the truck (Na 2 Kha 492) evaded the Birganj Customs Office, the police personnel tried to stop and take control of the truck laden with steel utensils whereas the APF personnel who were escorting the consignment, however, protested the police intervention, thus ending up in a clash[6]. According to reports, it was found that the APF and the importing agency were involved in manipulating Custom Duty[7]. There are many such incidents that show the clues for those who want to manipulate border management and take undue advantages.

Inequality

Inequality has become another major hurdle to maintain Nepal-India border free of smuggling. As mentioned elsewhere, many goods are smuggled due to price differences. If something is available in cheaper rate on the other side of the border, almost all prefer to cross the border for getting them in cheap price. It's human nature, and will be difficult for the security agencies to control it. While we are in the field, we tried to compare the local market prices in both sides of the border, and found a huge gap in price. For example, per KG onion price in Nepal side of Bhittamod (Mahottari) was almost double than the price in Indian side. If one saves 20 rupees while buying a KG onion, he/she buys it by crossing the border. The same case was found in chemical fertilizer. One could save some 25 rupees if he/she buys DAP fertilizer from Indian market.

Non-uniform policy

There is lack of a uniform custom policy to manage local's movement: Though there is the single mechanism (SSB and APF as frontier security supported by general police and intelligence bureaus of both the countries)

---

6 For details, Ravi Dahal, "Police forces clash over truck smuggling utensils", *The Himalayan Times*, August 3, 2013.

7 Bhusan Yadav, "Sasastra Ko Samrakshyan Ma Taskari Bhayeko Khulasa (Discloser of a smuggling under the Protection of Armed Police Force", *Kantipur* Daily, August 7, 2013

deployed in the entire Nepal-India border, different policies have been found in different points while implementing. It was observed that there was noa uniform policy but it would be much dependent on a person or a team deployed in the border. The border point would be tightened for locals all of a sudden along with the change of a team or even a commander there. It was basically the case for Police and SSB command. For example, Birganj/Raxaul border had been tightened while Ramesh Kharel was posted as SP. That was also the case in the Indian side. "Once new officer came as SSB commander (Assistant Commander), the whole SSB were defamed due to his involvement in corruption", some of the Rupaidiya-based journalists told the team during a group discussion. "We find no stable policy that regulates the border. If there is someone on duty, he/she allows us to carry household goods without any hassle. But that would not be the case after change of the duty officer as she/he imposed his/her own rules," argued the locals. During our visits to bordering areas, such policy differences were found quite often. Some border points allowed locals to carry sugar, rice and other household goods in a sufficient manner- sufficient for a family at least for 15 days. But some of the border points were not flexible enough for same thing. "It depends upon person to person (who is in duty). We need 2-4 quintal of sugar, and some 50-70 litres of oil/ghee to celebrate somebody's Sraddha (death anniversary) here in our locality. But SSB started controlling the amount to carry from other side of border. They say they can allow only 15-20 KG sugar and 5-7 litres of oil/ghee for the function which is insufficient," Bindeshwar Yadav, Dinesh Yadav and Shambhu Sah of Kacharwa-7, Bara told the research team in one of the group discussions[8]. "This border is no more an open border. There is a ban imposed even in bringing household goods in small scale. Let us take Santapur (Ilam) as an example where people can not cross the border with household goods. It has been banned. Even Pashupatinagar used to be one of the main custom points till recently. But India has blocked this border since 2007. There is no transaction of goods," Lila Shrestha of Pashupatinagar tells the team.

Such a policy variation was found not only in limiting access to household goods, but also to human movement. We have witnessed the following practices which are not pan - border phenomenon but the area specific innovations of Nepal-India border.

---

8   Research team's discussion with the locals, April 21, 2013.

Causes Behind The Border Related Problems: An Analysis

- Pashupati (Pashupatinagar) check point of Indian immigration office has been maintaining a record of human movement. Though the 3rd country citizen cannot use the border point, the Indian immigration and custom request both the Nepalese and Indian citizens to register their names while crossing the border. They have hung two boards (One in Nepali and another in English) in their office walls saying that "Nepalese/Indian citizens entry here." It is unique characteristic of this particular border, which we found nowhere in other points of Nepal_ India border.

- The Banbasa border crossing point is considered as one of the busiest and probably the most notorious of the transit points between two countries. It is due to two reasons; the first was that the Banbasa border opens only five hours a day. Since there is fixed time to use it, hundreds of travellers line up in order to wait the time in both the sides of the border. Secondly, it is the only border we have observed so far where India has two separate checkpoints within a distance of about 250 metres. If you are entering Nepal, your luggage is searched by Indian policemen first. Then you are allowed to cross the bridge over the Mahakali River. Soon after crossing the bridge will come another checkpoint operated by Custom, SSB and India's border security force along the border with Nepal. It is said that this unique and controversial check post came into existence a few years ago almost overnight provoking much anger from the Nepali population[9].

- Another unique phenomenon we observed was the gate system in the bordering area. We have found that the two border points- Jhulaghat and Dharchula-Darchula are opened for public for 12-13 hours per day only (From 6 am to 6 pm during the winter and 6-7 in the summer). More surprising practice one could find in these border points was the practice of door system in the suspension bridge. Once it is time to close, security apparatus of both the countries close the door together in coordination. By doing so, they want to make sure that there is no human movement beyond the fixed time. We don't understand the reasons behind it, but we have observed that the locals have been suffering badly due to this

---

9   See in details, http://www.ekantipur.com/the-kathmandu-post/2010/10/25/related_articles/crossing-the-line/214139.html, accessed by author on September 20, 2013.

practice. Just one day before our team was in Dharchula, a person had to spend more than three hours on the bridge due to the lack of coordination of the two security apparatus deployed there. One person who had to go towards India reached the Indian border point at around 6.15, just after the doors were closed. As per his request, Nepali security guard opened the gate and allowed him to go to the other side of the border. Once he entered through the gate, they locked the door and went back to their station. But once he reached the gate of the Indian side, the SSB guard didn't open the gate. Then, he had no option except to spend hours on the suspension bridge. Eventually, he was rescued around 10.00 pm once he was seen by one of the SSB commanders while roaming. These are the cases one often sees in Nepal-India border points.

> Why such a practice of operating the gates? Has it helped to control unwanted activities? The answer would be "No". Due to such a practice, local people who are getting used to swimming the Mahakali river cross the border without being noticed by the security guards. "Even if the gate is closed, people smuggle many things by using the narrow part of Mahakali River," a Custom official in charge of Khalanga, Darchula says.

> It has been observed in September 2013[10] that the SSB in Rupaidiya stalled a shed in front of its camp and started searching laguages carried by each and every traveller. But , it was not the case. during our fieldvisit in December.

Revenue collection

Last, but not the least, the problematic issue we have observed was Nepal's priority on revenue collection. Many Nepalese Custom officers deployed in Nepal-India border acknowledged that Nepal has priority in collecting revenue at any cost. "We have to convince our seniors, and collecting more and more revenue is only the way to do so. But Nepali government has to realize that only the amount should not be the criterion to rate one Custom's performance," many Custom officers say. "If it is only the fixed criterion, one could encourage people to smuggle goods from Indian side so that he/she meets the target of revenue," one of the Custom officers states. "Nepali

---

10 During the follow up fieldwork starting from September 14-17, 2013.

Causes Behind The Border Related Problems: An Analysis

state has focused on revenue. While doing so, we have to compromise in many aspects i.e. relations with the counterparts, humanitarian ground etc. which should not be the case between two very friendly nations and people," Narad Gautam, Chief Custom Officer of Krishnanagar states. Interestingly, we have observed a couple of scenarios as refereed by the Custom officers. But, even if the custom officials of Nepal argue about Nepal's revenue collection priority, there is a strong argument about the loss of revenue while importing goods and materials. It is said that there is a huge loss of revenue due to manipulation of Nepal's custom regime. Since Nepali custom don't accept invoices issued in India, smugglers and businessmen save a big amount of money (which should be the revenue of Nepali state) by under invoicing or wrong billing of imported items. "Nepal Customs don't accept invoices issues by Indian market. Neither have they relied on our (Indian) Custom's documents. Rather it allows custom officer and importer to price the items. I think, Nepal is losing a big amount of revenue out of this practice," Ashutosh Agarwal[11], Consul General of India, shares his suspicions with the research team. Once one import goods with under invoicing in the custom, he/she will try his/her best to save more money by selling it in the market without VAT bills. That is how businessmen are making more and more profit in Nepal.

In Nepalganj border, we could observe many women and children involved in carrying goods like lentil, sugar, rice etc. These were the goods Indian government had banned to export. Once we follow the carriers, we found two tented stores (*Godam*) within 300 meters of the border. It was surprising to see those stores situated just behind Nepali Custom office of Janunaha (Neplaganj) where they collect all the smuggled goods from women and children paying them 50 rupees per trip. But it was made easy and possible due to Nepali sates' policy fault. What we have observed was that the tent owners put these goods in a nicely printed bag,with proper packing. Once collected goods for a truckload, they make all necessary documents, pay the custom duty to the Nepal government and supply these things to different cities of Nepal as if it is all imported from Rupaidiya. More interesting scenario was witnessed in Matihani Sub-Custom Office. Once we visited the office, we have seen more than a dozen of plastic bags with rice inside the office. Since the bags were not sealed properly, one of us asked the duty officer about it. According to him, somebody (carrier) has stored the rice bags over there, and he will pay custom and import it to

---

11 Based on researchers discussion with Agarwal, October 6, 2013.

Nepal once there are 50-60 bags. The SSB don't allow carrying it unless one destroys the seal of bags. That is why they do like this", the Officer states.[12] Once we discussed with the Chief Custom Officer of Banke, he replied that they have provision to check and control the goods coming from the 3rd countries but without legal provision to check and control if goods are coming from Nepal to India. "Goods coming from Nepal and India will be considered as local, and we have no rights to verify whether it is coming from Nepal or not. That is why we allow those goods by taking the necessary custom duty," the Chief says. Due to such mentality of Nepali state, Nepali officers and public have to listen to grievances by Indian counterparts. "It's strange to be in the custom point of the Nepal side where there is no counterpart office available in Indian side. I think we should either request Indians to open Custom office on their side or close our office as well. Otherwise, it will help damage our relations with India," one Custom Staff deployed in Nepali side of the Custom says. Along with him, there were many who felt a need to not only reopen the custom points along with Custom Office which were open till recently and now closed due to many reasons, but also to reopen more border points. According them, that helps avoid people's pretext to say that they were compelled to use porous area of the border due to the long distance of Custom Check Point. "There were a couple of Chhoti Bhansars (sub-Custom offices) in Bardiya till recently. But those which were stopped due to Maoist conflict are yet to be reopened. Only a Gulway Chhoti Bhansar is there in Rajapur. People find no place even if they are ready to pay Custom," SP of APF Bardiya states.

Media often reports how people are suffering due to lack of custom offices. However, officers of Department of Customs don't accept the allegation saying that no Custom Office was closed. "There are 31 main Custom offices and 143 sub- offices at various border-crossing points", they say[13]. "Due to security reasons, some of the staffs left the sub-Custom Offices and started working from the main offices. But we have not closed any such office" Ram Prasad Sharma of Department of Customs, Kathmandu states[14].

---

12 Based on Field Obsevation, October 7, 2013.

13 Since it is their official position, it has been published in their recent document as well. For details, see Department of Customs ' Customs Reform & Modernization Strategies and Action Plan (CRMSAP) 2013 to 2017.p.1.

14 Researchers' discussion with Sharma, September 21, 2013.

Causes Behind The Border Related Problems: An Analysis

According to the official website of Custom Department of Nepal,[15] there are 20 Custom Offices along the border with India, and the sub-customs offices i.e. Bhadrapur, Thadi, Viswa, Mahehspur, Suthouli, Prithivipur, Sati, Gularia and Darchula are also authorized to trade with India. However, we could observe many sub-custom offices other than mentioned in the website during our fieldwork;but many of them were in a similar situation as mentioned by Sharma. For example, a signboard of sub-Custom office was seen in Jhulanipur (near Gandak hydropower) of Nawalparasi district. Once we tried to discuss with the officials there, we came to know that it was no more operational as there are no one except a peon in the office. Similar Situation was witnessed in Baladiya (Dhanusha, Nepal, near Nagar, Bihar) where a sub-custom existed without any staff.

Apart from such points mentioned before, another problem seems to have been created not due to real problem they face but due to their high expectation taking it as international boundary and expecting the state treatment accordingly. In other words, sometimes,, we felt that people wanted undue advantage after crossing the border, and become critical once they were not given proper attention by the people and government of India. Generally it is right that one should get special attention once he/she is in abroad. But due to the various facts- the exodus of people, common physical features etc., it becomes impossible for providing such special treatment to peoples of Nepal and India. Not only the common people who cross the border for their daily needs but also the truck drivers, businessmen, traders expect especial treatment. Once the state fails to do so, they get irritated and start criticizing the neighbour. Many people we talked during our fieldwork raised some issues in a very prominent manner without realising that these are very general issues and can be often witnessed at local level. For example, charging high fare by the private vehicles, taking more profits by businessmen, loot, robbery, bribe taking by local polices and government officers are the common issues available in both the countries. But if a Nepali citizen faces one such problem in India, he/she forgets the similar situation of his/her country. The Indians also have similar feeling but their feelings do not get much prominence in the media.

We are not arguing that there were no cases in which citizens of neighbouring state were not being targeted. One often finds that many

---

15 http://customs.gov.np/faq/giac.php

Nepalese had to face difficult situation due to his/her being Nepali and many Indians suffered in Nepal due to their Indian identity. Firstly, once they cross border, they become weak and vulnerable as they don't know who their friend is and who is enemy.

But it is common in each and every society that there are some anti-social elements to take undue advantage of such vulnerability. Basically such cases have become major problems of Nepal-India border. Once there is link of government agencies and such anti-social elements due to some monetary interest, it becomes disastrous. Likewise, such anti-social element treats some unavoidable incidents like traffic accident in different manner so that they get undue advantages. Our respondents of Rupaidia discussion also hinted at similar problems and stated "Indian four wheelers, 10 wheelers, when found committing small mistake in Nepalese road, are harassed, exploited and physically assaulted by Nepalese traffic police officers and local people. They are charged money unnecessarily. Suppose if an Indian number plate vehicle is running on Nepalese road touches a Nepalese vehicle, the reaction from Nepalese side is violent. What we often hear is 10-12 local people gather and torture the vehicle staffs inhumanly." Here, Sahabuddin Musalman's case may be worth mentioning. He, who is permanent resident of Gurgaun of Hariyana, was beaten up by two Nepalese youths in Nawalparasi while he was driving back from Kathmandu to Bhairahawa. The reason behind the incident was that his denial to pay money in Thumsi Dhat (blockade for collecting money).

According to a report, he who paid 50 Indian Rupees as fee while going towards Kathmandu was asked for 200 Rupees on his way back. Since they gave no receipt for the money, he denied paying it saying that he doesn't have that much amount[16]. Similar cases can be observed in Indian side as well. In fact, the Nepal – India border is one of the very few in South Asia where the trucks of one country can cross the border and operate in the other. Indian trucks can enter Nepal duty free for 72 hours to deliver cargo. But according to Musalman, he paid tax in about 10 spots starting from Belahiya of Rupandehi to Thankot of Kathmandu. People state that similar situation has to be faced by Nepalese vehicles if we travel to Indian side with Nepalese number plate vehicle. "Indians are daring to drive with their vehicle as their voices are being heard by their government and report to Nepal government if something was wrong with them in Nepal.

---

16 *Dainik* Patrika, May 12, 2013.

Causes Behind The Border Related Problems: An Analysis

We Nepalese rarely do it as it is risky and our government is inefficient in addressing such problems faced by its citizen," Bamdev Neupane, a boarding owner of Nepalganj states[17]. However, there are other issues as well. It has been reported that the 72 hours provision which is sufficient for the Indian trucks to drive to Kathmandu, unload and return to the border, is not sufficient for Nepalese trucks to operate in India, beyond the nearest town/railhead. That is why one cannot see Nepali trucks in India except a few trucks carrying transit cargo to/from Kolkata. It is said that it is partly the "result of the ultimate destination being beyond the 72 hour operating limit", and mainly, it is the "result of problems/costs caused by the Indian state authorities"[18]. For example, some areas in India, drivers avoid travelling at night due to poor security but if a truck exceeds 72 hours limit, this becomes a pretext collecting additional money from the vehicles. More so, what we have observed is different. In case of Indian vehicles (cars and vans), are concerned, they get free passes if they want to visit local markets of Nepali side and go back to India on the same day. But they have to pay certain fee (now 452 Nepali Rupees per day), if they want to spend nights in Nepal. All these processes will be made by Nepali Custom Offices available in the Nepal-India border. But for Nepali vehicles, it has to follow slightly different procedure. If a Nepali vehicle wants to go to Indian cities, it has to: (1) get permits issued by either Indian Embassy to Nepal or by its Consulate Offices, (2) In issuing the permit, the vehicle owner has to submit not only vehicle related documents and driving licence, but also Bank Guarantee, (3) It has to wait at least a day to receive the permit. These three provisions seem to have made difficult for Nepalese vehicles to go to Indian cities as these are not the cases for Indian vehicles coming to Nepal. While discussing with Ashutosh Agarwal (CG), it is known that India has imposed those conditions in a different context, and it has now started working to ease the process[19].

Compared to opportunities, less or no burdens are created by Indo-Nepal border. Some of the following aspects are worth noticing:

> ➢ One of the biggest burdens of open border is that stolen vehicles especially motorbikes are sold across the border in both sides.

---

17 Discussion with researchers on September 16, 2013.

18 Sanjib Pohit, "Overview of India-Nepal Trade: Trends, Trade Logistics and Impediments", MPRA Paper No. 45874, 2009.

19 Based on researchers discussion with Agarwal, October 6, 2013.

Once something is lost, it will soon be taken across border in India and then after, there is no chance of finding it.

➤ The other drawback of open border is that there is smuggling of consumable goods by individuals for business men. Goods are smuggled evading custom duty and sold at high prices in Nepalese market.

The poor Nepalese workers returning from India after seasonal work are charged more than the stipulated fare by Tanga and Rickshaw owners. It has been a big issue in Western Nepal, especially in Gourifanta and Banbasha borders. Rikshaw pullers gang up to loot people. 40-50 Rikshaw drivers have made a nexus to carry only those labourers who come all the way from big cities in India. They won't allow other Rikshaws to take such passengers. They not only stop others from taking passengers but also cheat passengers by charging high rate. Sometimes, they urge passengers to pay more so that they escape possible hindrances at the airport. (Generally Rikshaw charges 30-40 Rs from the Gaurifanta boarder to Bus park, but once we verified those Rikshaws charge 300-400 for the early morning passengers). A journalist states that he tried to bring this news to public notice. But the nexus called for strike and Chakkajam. Eventually, local administration had to succumbed to their pressure[20]. Similar case is found in Banbasa border. They cheat mostly the people when they know that people come back with earning. According to Manoj Khatri of Banbasa Immigration office, Nepali Maoist takes money out of passengers travelling from and to Mahendranagar. That is the reason why Maoists help Tanga to continue. "Tangas take not only high fare but also extra money saying that they have a deal with Custom, SSB etc. to avoid checking up the bags and unnecessary harassments. Border authority tried to introduce bus services up to the Nepal border but had to withdraw the plan due to local's pressure", he states. Bijay Pant, a local of Mahendranagar shares his own experience and states "I once tried to run buses from Mahendranagar to Delhi. I had offered very cheap fare on the route (Mahendranagar-Delhi-Mahendranagar), but I could not get permission by the authority. I know a kind of nexus between Rikshaw drivers, owners and Mahendranagar Municipality staffs. Though all Rikshaws belong to Indian owners, they are

---

20 In Gaurifanta, that was the case mentioned by the locals while we were conducting field study. But now the government has introduced a city bus service up to the border (Follow up fieldwork, September 14-17, 2013).

Causes Behind The Border Related Problems: An Analysis

registered in Municipality under the names of Nepalese who are relatives of Municipality staffs", he states. According to him, Municipality staffs get 800 a month from a Tanga as commission.

One of the main problems in crossing the border is that the roads especially in the border region in Indian side are very bumpy and are not maintained; this creates a problem for goods transport and transfer of sick patients who cross the border for treatment. The following expression by a prominent Indian scholar C. Rajamohan[21] provides a clue to the real situation of the bordering area:

> Entering Raxaul in Bihar from Birganj in Nepal, one moves from the third world to the fourth. New Delhi might fancy itself as one of the world's most dynamic economies and an emerging great power. At Raxaul, you would not know. There is nothing "shining" about India here… India's official institutions on this border are naked amid the prevailing anarchy. There is not even a small notice saying you are on Indian soil. The all-enveloping chaos is proof-enough that you are in "incredible India"! Trucks, oil tankers and bullock carts have jammed up what you can barely call a road. One of the main arteries of trade between India and Nepal is now a long stretch of mud and potholes at Raxaul. If its institutions on the borders define a nation-state, Raxaul reflects the profound decay in India's border management…The Indo-Nepal border might be free in theory. But commerce does not flow easily across it — thanks to the obstacle race that the infrastructure on the Indian side has become.

Though Rajamohan admired Nepali side of the border saying that there is some dignity, including an arched gateway welcoming visitors. Yet the infrastructure of Nepal also has become very poor in recent years.

Along with the poor infrastructure in bordering area, there is also a lack of government monitored traffic management units . Due to their absence, locals have monopoly in the market. That is what is happening in Nepal-India border which resulted in public harassment and cheating. The following seems to be an interesting event.

> Early in the morning at 6.49, dozens of people gathered in the Indian side searching vehicle to go to the NJP station and Siligiri. One

---

21 http://www.hindu.com/2003/12/24/stories/2003122403751200.htm

full cab along with 7 passengers arrived there crossing the security. It was stopped by a mob of vehicle racketeers. Though the cab was going towards Siliguri, but was not allowed to go. The argument was that it has violated rules set by the locals. They argue that the cab driver went towards Nepal just to take passengers though he was arguing that his vehicle lacks fuel so that he is allowed to move ahead. Eventually the mob took the key of the cab away from the driver, and compelled passengers to leave the vehicle. Though it is tussle between the local taxi owners, what people feel is more important. While getting down from the vehicle, all passengers were in angry mood though only a few spoke there.

As stated earlier, such incident is due to the tussle of local taxi owners, and India and Indian security has nothing to do with such things, but blames goes to India and Indians. This is how common people start developing negativism against neighbour. If there was government mechanism to regularize the transporters, it would have controlled the damage by providing good service. During our field visits, we have observed similar situation, couple of which provides a clue to say that Nepal-India border has been a neglected area. Gourifanta border has no option except to remain in temporary sheds. There is neither office building nor even access to Indian Telephone network. That is why most of the Indian personnel deployed in the bordering areas use Nepali mobile network as they have to rely on Nepali mobile. It is said that some people from some 45 villages (right from Tikunia in the east to Banbasa in the west) of Indian side of the border use Nepali mobile networks[22]. Such dependency of Indian border security is found not only in Gourifanta but also in Nepalganj of Banke, Pashupatinagar of Ilam, and Ganeshpur-Balegaun bordering area of Bardiya. While we visited Pashupatinagar, most of the Indian border staffs i.e. custom officer, immigration officer and police offers were taking tea on the Nepal side, whereas in Nepalganj case, most SSB and Indian custom officers were found dependent on Nepali mobile network. More than the mobile network, SSB persons deployed in the western parts of Nepal-India border have no option except to use the Nepal's market. For example, those who are deployed in Ganeshpur-Balegaun bordering area of Bardiya have to travel 4 kilometres to reach Kalabazaar (the nearest Indian market) where it is only 800 meters for them to reach Nepali market. "Most of bordering areas of India side are covered by dense forest. That is why

---

22 *Morning Bell* Nepali Daily, October 7, 2012.

Causes Behind The Border Related Problems: An Analysis

SSB has no easy access to Indian market. Dependency also help create a harmonious relationship," Rishi Dev Karki, SP of Bardiya APF states[23].

As far as Nepal's dependency is concerned, obviously Nepali security is not the exceptional case. But some of the cases seem to be extreme for Nepalese officers managing the bordering area. For example, most Nepali officials deployed in Jhulaghat border (Baitadi) have no place to reside in Nepali side. That is why they rent house in Indian side of the border to live. "You can imagine what kind of morale an official has who has to take shelter in the foreign land before and after the office hour", Lokendra Rai, Custom Officer of Jhulaghat bemoans.

Nepal, being one of the poorest countries, may have some pretext not to provide adequate facility to its officials. But once one observes the kind of poor infrastructure on Indian side, he or she concludes that India's border management mechanism is also one of the neglected areas that helped demoralize those officers deployed there. When our study team visited Indian Police Post in Bhittamod, we were surprised to see the conditions of the office. We saw no one in official dress and found difficulty to identify the officials. Interestingly, we asked a person, sitting on a cot under a hut, disclosed his identity as a DSP of Bihar Police. Once we started discussing about the border issue, he had to elaborate the poor conditions of his office and residence of staffs. "We are shy enough to mention us as senior officials of Indian (Bihar) police as we are operating our office in this condition", one of the officials says during our conversation. Robbery was a major threat of the border area in the past. But, now, there are no such problems because of the presence of SSB and APF. But still criminals and smugglers flee to other side of border once they have committed crime. Crimes of personal rivalry and contract assignments do take place on both sides and the open border gives the advantage to criminals to flee to other side of borders and start a normal life with no fears of arrests or prosecution. Regular news of abduction and killings are reported where mostly cross border criminals are involved. Though some crimes have been controlled by stationing of SSB and APF, still poor Nepalese people returning from work with their limited savings face harassment from SSB and Indian Custom authorities. It is reported that the nexus of border personnel and local Rishaw pullers/ Tanga conductors unnecessarily collect money in order to bribe the inspectors for avoiding checking of people's luggage and Indian currency

---

23 As per discussion with research team on January 2, 2013.

notes of 500 and 1000.

Also it is often reported that the Indian vehicles are being unnecessarily levied duty in Nepal even if they cross border following the rules and regulations. During the fieldwork,, we have seen a staff of the Nepali Custom Office, Kailali, who was on duty, charging 50 rupees per vehicle while issuing a day-long pass for Indian vehicles. According to the policy, Indian vehicle can spend a couple of hours in the bordering markets and go back to India in the evening. For daily permission, no charge has to be paid. Apart from custom, vehicles which use Gaurifanta border to come to Nepal have to pay local tax twice to the District Development Committees of Nepal. Interestingly, the distance of these two-tax collecting booths are hardly 150 meters. Once one enters into Nepal, he/she touch the Kanchanpur District, and will reach Kailali District after crossing some 100 meters. There is a small river to divide two districts which is quite genuine. However, why should a foreigner need to understand it? He or she may see it differently as if it is the strategy to collect revenue for the local body.

In summary, people from both, India and Nepal, living in bordering areas, consider the open border as an economic opportunity. Basically, the opportunities are explained in employment and business. In case of employment, people from both sides, Nepal and India, seem to be working on either side. However, the employment opportunities are sporadic/seasonal and not of regular type. While considering business as another opportunity, people from India seem to be making the most out of the border relation in comparison to people from Nepal. Daily, a lot of people from Nepal visit Indian markets to buy goods, clothes, equipment, etc. It can be said that border markets are basically targeted for the Nepalese people rather than the native Indians. Most selling business and cross border transport is owned by Indians. The sale includes daily used house hold commodities of edible items, utensils, fabrics, decorative items, fruits and vegetables. Nepalese go to buy such items at a cheaper price than in Nepal. Most of the cross border transport business is also owned by Indians.

Chapter VII : Conclusion, Observations and Suggestions

In fact, Nepal-India open border is a life line for those living on either side. However, political, academic and expert discourses of the capitals of both the countries try to undermine the relevance and significant of Nepal-India open border. Yes, there are some unwanted incidents by certain miscreants which cannot be rule out. In other words, Nepal-India border is not a problem-free area due to multidimensional relations existing between the two countries for centuries. It does not mean that the outstanding problems that recur due to open border should not be tackled or addressed from time to time. Many border related problems were pilled up due to the inability to hold higher level meetings i.e. Nepal-India Joint Commission with authority to resolve the dispute.

However, it seems that Prime Minister Narendra Modi's visit to Nepal in August 2014 had generated more hopes as it was significant in many respects, including the border dispute within two countries. Before the PM Modi's visit, Sushma Swaraj, Minister of External Affairs, visited Nepal to attend the Joint Commission Meeting (JCM) on July 2015. The JCM meeting which had taken place after 23 years gap largely agreed to further "reinvigorate" the relationship by stepping up engagement in new areas. It was the meeting which decided on setting up an Eminent Persons Group to identify new areas of cooperation and suggest measures to help both the countries seize all possible opportunities. The JCM also specifically deliberated on issues relating to defence and security and agreed to expand cooperation. The overall sense of the deliberation was that "security of both the countries was intertwined". Both the countries have agreed to the terms of reference for setting up of the group. It was decided that the Foreign Secretary level mechanism would work on the outstanding Boundary issues including Susta and Kalapani on priority basis, taking technical inputs from BWG, as necessary. Following the decision, the first meeting of the India-Nepal BWG was held in Kathmandu from 17-19 September 2014 to discuss matters relating to repair, reconstruction and maintenance of boundary pillars on the India-Nepal border. The two delegations were led by the respective Surveyor Generals of the two countries. The meeting agreed to install the global positioning system (GPS) in every boundary pillar between the two countries in a bid to avoid future disputes on pillar location and to expedite reinstallation of the structures with pinpoint accuracy. All the 8,553 pillars on Nepal-India border are to be fitted with the GPS system with the information of longitude, latitude, height and geographical location, and monitored with the help of 83 control points. The two countries have also agreed to construct special pillars in the middle of rivers, streams and dense forests. Also, the second Nepal-India BWG meeting at the surveyor general-level was held in Dehradun, India, on August 26-27 2015 to prepare guidelines for the survey official's committee responsible for undertaking the construction, restoration and repair, clearing the 'no-man's land' except in the two disputed areas.

Also, Modi could create positive feeling after his twenty four hour visit and his address to the Nepali parliament. On the one hand, no Indian Prime Ministers had visited for seventeen years, despite the innumerable visits by the Nepali side on the other; Modi could assuage the feeling of distrust by addressing Nepal's important concerns including trade and investment. He also at length dealt with the entire gamut of Nepal-India relations as if he was making a departure from the past policies. His reference to Nepal as the land of Buddha and bilateral ties based on open border made Nepali satisfied. However, such bonhomie did not change the structural relationship, nor did he make any fresh bid for changing the substantive part of relationship.

Prime Minister Modi declared in parliament that India would provide one billion dollar soft loan to help build infrastructure in Nepal. He assured that the work on Pancheswar multipurpose hydropower project would begin in a year committing to prepare a detailed project report within six months. Memorandum of Understanding (MoU) was signed on tourism development, Goitre control program in Nepal, in addition to many other projects relating to communication and hydropower. Following the Prime Minister's initiative, India and Nepal signed 10 pacts on 25 November 2014 during his second visit to Nepal that he undertook for attending the SAARC summit held in Kathmandu. The pacts included five Agreements

CONCLUSION, OBSERVATIONS AND SUGGESTIONS

and five MoUs which are:

List of five agreements that were lined to:

- Agreement on extending Line-of-Credit of 1 billion US dollar by India
- Motor Vehicle Agreement (MVA)
- Twin City Agreement between Ayodhya – Janakpur
- Twin City Agreement between Kathmandu – Varanasi
- Twin City Agreement between Lumbini – Bodh Gaya

The other list containing the MOUs were as follows:

- MoU on Nepal Police Academy (NPA)
- MoU on Tourism
- MoU Traditional Medicines
- MoU on Youth Exchange
- MoU on PDA for ARUN III

The present study based on field works and meeting with common peoples living in the bordering areas found some issues that need to be addressed on a regular basis by the two sides. And some of these areas which are also discussed before are the following:

1. Agreements reached since the signing of the Sugauli Treaty (1815-16) to the present have outlined the contours of Nepal-India relations, though civilization links go back to distant past. Some Nepalis hold the view that some of the treaties have compromised Nepal's independence as a sovereign nation and hence necessity of adjusting them to the present time. Sometimes, the treaties, specially the 1950 Treaty, are singled out for criticism. Theoretically, their opinion might be valid, but in the domain of real politic, treaties that guide the relations need to be objectively assessed. Many other developed states have similar treaty relations with powerful states as the realist practitioners think that such formal arrangements have not obstructed the development of the country.

Nor could any country be, inter alia, independent in today's world as nations are increasingly becoming more interdependent in their regular interactions.

2. The open border and the 1950 Treaty are inseparable as the clause pertaining to the movement of peoples , the same kind of treatment to be meted out to the nationals of both the countries as per the treaty provision is guaranteed by this instrument, though the erosion of the treaty is another reality. Legal provisions, courts' interpretations and public pressures for safeguarding the interests of respective countries have given rise to elites' misconception and misunderstanding. Politicians, who tend to swing according to perceptions, if not reality, have often generated controversies on the actual functioning of the treaty. So in Nepal-India relations, perception is as much dominant as reality.

3. Open border management needs to be addressed with a two-pronged strategy: state to state mechanisms and greater understanding of the subject. The state level mechanisms have also unilateral and bilateral components. Internally, each contracting state develops its own measures for controlling, regulating and maintaining border areas. Nepal and India have realized such mechanism when both the countries have handed over the charge of border maintenance to the SSB (India) and APF (Nepal). In addition, administrators and custom officials and other related organs hold occasional joint meetings either in India or Nepal. They have put in place such mechanisms that oversee the overall border related problems. It has been said that except the three disputed borders — Kalapani, Susta and Pashupatinagar (Fatak) Ilam, other related problems have been settled. Yet, no formal agreement on the settled border issue is officially signed. What is the hitch behind it is not yet known to general people. Nevertheless, in a joint meeting of the two sides held in Kathmandu on June 1, 2013 both sides have taken up forming a new technical team to complete the mapping of the remaining parts of Nepal - India border. The meeting decided to form a new panel to map the remaining Susta and Kalapani areas, to maintain boundary pillars and to demarcate the boundary according to the agreed strip maps. Both the governments need to realize the fact that most

Conclusion, Observations and Suggestions

of the problems were outcomes of the border dispute, and once the dispute is addressed by two neighbors, many problem will be resolved.

It can be suggested that border on the whole can be demarcated on longitude-latitude basis. This approach will immediately find out the border even if the rivers change their course or pillars disappear. It is also river-neutral. It can be managed by the local authorities of two sides.

4. The Nepali APF has no mandate to safeguard the Hill areas except a few border points. Some Police personnel seem to regulate, though in some points such as Taplejung, Panchthar and Darchula, police stations are far away from the border. It takes time two- three days to reach the border, while the Indian SSB is present in all posts. Lack of resources and scant attention paid to the minimum needs of security personnel has affected the effective management of border in the remote hill areas of Nepal.

5. Security is intimately connected with custom, drug trafficking and movement of peoples of both countries. It is also said that "law enforcement personnel of both sides get tempted to take personal, financial, and material gain. Such trends are ignored as long as it serves the interest of local people and petty local politicians. It has been a long tradition to shelter small or big criminals wanted by India in Nepal and vice -versa who feel safe and invincible because they are protected under political shield or buy their safety from political and security agencies"[1].

6. Security is the main concern of India. That Nepal being used as a safe haven for dreaded terrorists has added significance. The arrest of Syed Abdul Karim alias Tunda in Banbasha, India, and his disclosures of his links with the LeT have shown how terrorist groups operate by using open border. Nepal has cooperated in tracking down such dreaded terrorists and other criminals

---

1 Rabi Raj Thapa, retired Additional General of APF, has stated that " Indo-Nepal border breeds a cluster of national and international criminals whether they may be smugglers, drug traffickers, human traffickers, tax evaders, maiddlemen between government employees and the business manipulators, drivers and porters and so on". See Rabi Raj Thapa, " Prevention of Corss-Border Crime Along Nepal-India Borders" , *Souvenir* (Nepal-Bharat Maitri Samaj , Kathmandu, August , 2013),pp.79-81.

and handed over them to India. The Case of Sucha Singh in the early 1970s and Tunda's are, among many, examples, of mutual cooperation between the security forces of Nepal and India. International intelligence reports disclosed that Tunda used Kathmandu as a transit to India-Nepal border, but he was arrested in Nepal and handed over to Indian police in Mahendranagar – Banbasha border[2]. Similarly, another dreaded terrorist, Yasin Bhatkal, a founder of the terrorist outfit Indian Mujahideen, has been arrested from the Indo-Nepal bordering area. It has been stated by the high placed media sources that Bhatkal in fact was within Nepal and was detected by the Indian intelligence agencies in collaboration of Nepali police. Although such sources may lack veracity, the main point is that both Indian and Nepali security agencies have cooperated for controlling cross-country terrorist activities.

7. Security is a multidimensional issue having both national and international implications. Nationally, India faces armed groups in Nepal's neighbourhood, in Assam, Chhattisgarh, Jharkhand, Kashmir and in some pockets in Northeast. The Maoist violence is considered as a major threat to India's internal security. The use/misuse of open border by the terrorists in India or even of Nepal has posed security threats to both. And open border is often considered as the convenient location for cross-country terrorism. Moreover, the flight of refugees across the border is also a security problem area. For meeting such challenges, security agencies of both Nepal and India need to cooperate for tracking as well as arresting the criminals of all hues. Criminal gangs that operate along the Nepal-India border use the territories of both as safe haven. So only with a cooperative attitude on both sides, the state mechanisms can work effectively. Instead of scratching each other skin for minor issues that recur in bilateral relations, the two sides should consolidate their joint efforts for meeting the threat of

---

2 See the press reports of India and Nepal, August 6-19, 2013. See also *Times of India*, August 18,2013. As *Times of India* reports, " Delhi Police have arrested Abdul Karim Tunda, alias Abdul Quddooss, one of India's top 20 wanted terrorists, and mastermind of over 40 bombings in the country, from Indo-Nepal border". How Tunda used Kathmandu as a transit to travel to India by using the open India-Nepal border is also disclosed. See *Nagarik* daily(Kathmandu), August 27, 2013. For Yasin Bhatkal's arrest, see *Kathmandu Post* and the Hindu (New Delhi), August 30, 2013.

Conclusion, Observations and Suggestions

criminals, terrorists and other violent groups that thrive with the help of politicians and even of security agencies.

8. State mechanisms that operate on both sides and in cooperation with each other needs to be further augmented. The APF of Nepal, for instance, has limited mandate to regulate in addition to its manpower problem. In some places, at a distance of more than 25 km, no APF guard can be traced due to shortage of resources. On the Indian side, in less four km, SSB is stationed. However, in recent years, stationing of two forces along the border has contributed to controlling the border activities. What other measures can be adopted for minimizing security risks should be designed by both sides.

The second strategy is an understanding of the nature of relationship existing from time immemorial between Nepal and India. What are the compulsions of maintaining open border? Can the closure of border solve the bilateral problems? Can the peoples of both countries reconcile to ending the open border? What alternatives can be offered if the two countries decide to end the traditional relations? Can the open border arrangement as it exists today manage the emerging problems posed by a variety of factors that loom large in regional and international arena? What happens if the 1950 Treaty is abrogated without devising mutually agreed alternatives? Will India continue to absorb the Nepalis who find their way into India due to push factors such as natural calamities, insurgency, famine etc? Similarly what would be the fate of those Indians who have had been residing in Nepal or have been engaged in different kinds of works as skilled workers or raw human force?

9. Economic dimensions of bilateral relations are increasingly assuming significance when they encourage smuggling of all kinds of goods. Indulgence in illegal trade, evasion of tax system and promotion of criminal activities seem to be intermixed in the border. Nepali side is preoccupied with increasing revenue only and does not pay adequate attention to curbing the root causes of such economic aberrations. It can be proposed that a study of taxation system can find out some remedial measures. For it, both the governments should take initiative. It can also be proposed

that local level cooperation is a must in identifying criminals and people indulged in illegal economic transactions. Neighborhood watches scheme can be one of the measures for controlling criminal activities.

Radio communication along the bordering regions can also play an important role for educating the people about border issues. FM Radios can be encouraged to play such a role.

Such questions can be answered only with a deep understanding of the wide-ranging India-Nepal relations based on open border regime. Mere theoretical knowledge does not answer these questions. Nevertheless, if the two countries reach an understanding for changing the pattern of relations, then some alternative mechanisms can be devised for regulating the border. First, the public opinion should be created by political parties, media, intellectuals and others for making people understand the necessity of change. And it can be done through positive mind by shedding the old mindset for better bilateral relations. If the core policy makers of the two countries start working on a more cooperative relationship and if they get the backing of politicians regardless of parties, certain changes can be introduced. Indian security elites should also try to understand that more empathy is needed on both sides so that coordinated efforts could be made for preserving traditional relations along with the injection of a new confidence.

10. To make people better understand the nature of India-Nepal relations needs the revamped role of academic institutions where serious researches can be done and information disseminated. Knowledge can be imparted through good education as well as by the objective media. Research centres in India and Nepal can investigate into various areas and try to provide inputs to the general people, politicians and media. Media on its part should not only try to sensitize the issue but its reports should base on facts.

Quality school education can be provided to the children of people living near the border. Such education should be accessible to all, especially the children of poor people.

Conclusion, Observations and Suggestions

Culturally, Nepal and India can further increase their relations at people to level. Buddhist shrines and monuments can be popularized for promoting cultural tourism. Infrastructures of places of cultural importance can be developed for attracting more tourists. Wild-life parks can be created on the Nepali side of border for attacking greater number of tourists.

11. Terrorist activities, passage of arms or explosives or other material relating to security and now the drug trafficking and flow of fake Indian currencies by using China and Nepal as transit routes belong to the security zones. Similarly, flow of small arms into Nepal from India or use of border by criminals also comes under security domain. And the developing nexus between the politicians and criminals, who allegedly donate money and other logistics to the parties and politicians, create security threats. The open border has therefore become convenient for carrying out activities that pose threats to national security. Reports of smuggling of red sandal woods using Nepal as a transit country to China and the alleged involvement of security agencies in such deals often pour into the Nepali media.

12. Occasional complaints have been made on the movement of Armed Indian cops within the Nepali territory without prior information. In the wake of hot pursuits made against the criminals by the Indian police or other security agencies, news are circulated that they conduct the operations sometimes clandestinely and sometimes with the knowledge Nepali security agencies. On September 19, 2013, it was reported that a team of armed police personnel from India raided a house at Gulariya-8 in Bardiaya district. According to the media report, the Nepali Police was not informed in advance that such raid was underway in connection with the arrest of two criminals who had fled to Nepal after committing crime in India. It was confirmed that the criminals (killers of a policeman in India) were in fact had taken shelter in the house of Manjur Prasad Shrestha who stated that his friend in Lucknow requested him to take care of his friends during their visit to Bardiaya. But Shrestha maintained that he didn't know that they were the criminals from India. On being questioned how the Nepali police allowed them to return them after meeting them in Nepal, the police said that they escorted the Indian police team to the border on the order of

Mathi (from above)³. According to the Chief District Officer, the Indian police personnel were escorted to the border point in order not to scatter within Nepal.

The Indian Embassy in Nepal, by way of responding to the concern shown by the public as well as government, stated that that the Indian policemen would be taken to task if found guilty in going into Nepali territory without prior consultation with their Nepali counterparts.

It seemed that the India police personnel had come there after informing the APF (Nepal) and Nepali police. How the police could escort them to the border. Such incidents had taken place even in Kathmandu and elsewhere. Nepali security agencies have also handed over many criminals to India. Yet, both the governments should devise mechanisms to deal with criminals and terrorists who make Nepal-India border as entry and exit for their operations. Moreover, such incidents have often taken place as the Indian security agencies have apparently shown a lack confidence in Nepali authorities.

13. In order to minimize the occurrences of unauthorized entry of security forces of both the countries, a proper local level security coordination committee can be formed. Intelligence gathering and sharing needs to be further strengthened by both sides. Mutual trust, cooperation and coordination between securities agencies along the borders can help reduce the problems.

14. Political stability and effective governance are the two essential components of security, peace and development. Nepal has yet to settle its political direction. A lot of changes have taken place since the second mass movement of 2006. People have accepted republic, inclusive liberal democracy. Yet, the political forces have yet to lay the foundation of institutionalized democratic system along with the rapid economic development aiming at social justice. Unless the country is internally settled and develops confidence, relations with neighbours would also be under shadow.

---

3   See *The Kathmandu Post*, September 19, 2013.

Conclusion, Observations and Suggestions

15. Change in mindset of elites in both the countries would also help resolve many outstanding issues faced by the two countries. Such attitudinal change needs to come in hard core political and security elites. Feeling of good neighbourly relations based on equality, mutual respect, cooperation and understanding needs to be developed for strengthening relations.

Appendices

Appendix I

List of the people contacted/consulted during the fieldwork

1. Nabi Alamed, Jana Sandesh, Rupaidiya, India
2. Chandra Pal Singh Yadav, Police (civil), Rupaidiya, India
3. VK Yadav, SO/Uttar Pradesh Police, Rupaidiya, India
4. Aslam Khan, CD Nanpara ,9454401372
5. Karam Vir Singh, Constable, SSB, Rupaidiya, India
6. Samasuddhina Khan, Secretary, Panchayat, Kewalpur Gramfabha
7. PN Singh, Assistant Commander, SSB, Rupaidiya, India
8. Munni, Sub-inspector, SSB, Rupaidiya, India
9. Mani Ram Sarma, School teacher, Rupaidiya, India
10. Siraj Khan, Sadbhab Editor, 08-526168
11. Ramji Soni, Sprastha Aawaj
12. Bhagirath Chand, ASI, APF, Nepalganj, Nepal
13. Nirmal Dwivedi, Custom Officer, 7376541945
14. Kripa Sankar Pandey, SDM Nanpara, 9454416034
15. Arbind K. Mouria, Head Constable, immigration office
16. S.N Goswami, Constable, immigration office
17. Ganesh Balayar, SI of Armed Police, Chaulika chowck Seema Suraksha Karyalaya

18. Shiva Dhungana, Custom Office, Nepalganj 9856030978
19. Gopal Nath Yogee, Civil Society Member, Nepalganj
20. Dinesh Chaudhari, BEE Group
21. Jhalak Gaire, President, Federation of Nepali Journalists, Banke
22. Netra Panthi, BBC Nepali Sewa
23. Rishi Dev Karki, SSP, APF 9851012910
24. Arbind Chaudhary, Local, Gulairia
25. Resham Yadav, ASI, Nepal Police
26. Kabir Khan, local carrier of Indian side of Balegaun
27. Jagat Khan, local carrier of Indian side
28. Amrit Karki, Farmer of Nepali side of Jamunia
29. Jeet Nepali, Nepali farmer with cows and goats.
30. SSB personnel in Duty in Balugaun
31. Hawaldar in Duty, Nepal Police, Jamunia, Banke
32. Arbind Chaudhary, Local, Dhangadi
33. Anju Shrestha, Kurtha byapari, Chaurahi
34. Preeti Shakya, Gold Business, Nepali residence
35. Sourav Gupta, Pannalal and Sons, Dhangadi market
36. Hari Shankar Yadav, and Manoj Kumar, Constable, Gaurifanta (Lakhimpur Khari), Kotwali outpost
37. Kawarpal Singh, Kotwali
38. Jay Shanker Singh, Check Post Officer
39. V. B Singh, Custom Office, Gauriphanda
40. Sree Krishna Pandey, Gorakhpur, Wild Animal Guard
41. Ramesh Pandey, Gorakhpur, Forest Guard

Appendices

42. Naresh Pandey, government officer
43. Rawat, Editor Morning Bell (recorded)
44. Ram Thapaliya, CDO Kailali, 04-01-2013
45. Bhanudev Badu, Assistant CDO, Kailali
46. SSP Karki, Kailali, 9851280240
47. Abhimanu Das Mulmi, Road Division, 9851127679
48. Ganesh B.K, Civil Soceity Activist, Dhangadi
49. Karna Shah, Dhangadi Post, 9858420711
50. Santosh Agrawal, Rajestani origin businessmen in Dhangadi
51. Laxmi Bhandari, Inspector, Border
52. Dhan Prasad Sibakoti, Inspector, Narcotic Department, 9852670979
53. Sapan K. Chakma, ASI, SSB,
54. Buddiman Rai, SI, APF, Seema Surakshya, Kakarvitta
55. Balaram Pokharel, DSP, APF, Seema Surakshya, Jhapa
56. Anta Ram, Head Constable, Nepal Police
57. Anand Ghimire, Custom Office, Kakarvitta
58. Pankaj Sarkar, Sub-inspector, Immigration Office, Phoolbari, West Bengal
59. Dilip Kr. Barman, ASI, West Bangal Police outpost, Bagdora
60. Arun Roy, Police Constable, Traffic Police post, Phoolbari, WB
61. Prakash Phuyal, Assistant Editor, Siliguri
62. Rabin Koirala, UML Chairperson, Jhapa
63. Raju Sharma, Batike Hostel, Kakarvitta, Nepal
64. Balram Pokharel, DSP, Armed Police Force, Kakarvitta, Jhapa
65. Pashupati Khanal, Inspector, Armed Police Force, Kakarvitta, Jhapa, 9851071054

66. Basanta Tiwari, Mechi Uddyog Sangh/Custom Agent, Kakarvitta, Jhapa (FGD Participant)

67. Dinesh Pokhrel, Custom Agent, Kakarvitta, Jhapa (FGD Participant)

68. Santosh Sajil, Custom Agent, Kakarvitta, Jhapa (FGD Participant)

69. A teacher of Pashupati Boarding School, Kakarvitta, Jhapa (FGD Participant)

70. Representative of Maiti Nepal, Kakarvitta, Jhapa (FGD Participant)

71. Harka Rawal, SP, Armed Police Force, Bhadrapur Jhapa, 9855045125

72. Pandab Rajbanshi, SI, Nepal Police, Bhadrapur, Jhapa

73. Kumar Bahadur Koirala, Non-Gajatted officer, Custom office, Bhadrapur, Jhapa

74. Kishor Sapkota, Clerk, Custom office, Bhadrapur, Jhapa

75. Kunta Banset, Sanahaat, Bhadrapur, Jhapa

76. Anita Karki, Sanahaat, Bhadrapur, Jhapa

77. Chandra Bahadur Khadka, ASI, Armed Police Force, Bhadrapur Jhapa

78. Shiv Singh, SI, SSB, India, Galgalia, Bihar

79. Binup Mahoto, ASI, West Bengal Police, Raniganj, Khoribari

80. Pemba Bhutia, Inspector, Custom, Raniganj, Khoribari, India

81. Dhirendra Nath Sharma, Inspector, SSB , Pasupahtinagar, India

82. Surya Bahadur Shrestha, Custom Office, Pasupahtinagar, Nepal

83. Krishna Thami, Maiti Nepal, Pasupahtinagar, Nepal

84. Milan Chhetri, Proprietor, Hotel Seema, Pasupahtinagar,

APPENDICES

Nepal 9842635641

85. Saroj Dahal, Non-Gajatted officer, Custom office, Pasupahtinagar, Nepal

86. Lila Shrestha, Local Social Activist, Pasupahtinagar, Nepal 9851071549

87. Chudamani Khanal, Health Worker, Nepal Govt, Pasupahtinagar, Nepal

88. Gopal Pokheral, Pakali, Itahari,

89. Khadga Rai, Local, Pasupahtinagar, Nepal

90. Debendra Subba, Local, Pasupahtinagar, Nepal

91. Durga Bahadur Pradhan, ASI, Nepal Police, Biratnagar

92. Padma Bakadur B.K, ASI. Armed Police Force, Birat Nagar, Nepal

93. Sudeep Neupane, Police Constable, Nepal Police, Biratnagar

94. Bhagirath Regmi, Regional Police Office, Rani, Biratnagar

95. Mohan Lal Aga Shrestha, Sub-inspector, Rani, Birat Nagar, Nepal

96. L. B Basnet, Inspector, APF, Rani, Birat Nagar, Nepal

97. Raghav Singh Thapa, SP, Armed Police Force, Morang, Nepal

98. Kamal Subba, Biratnagar Bhansar Sewa Mahasangha (BBSM)

99. Lekhnath Bahal, Advisor, BBSM, Biratnagar, Nepal

100. Shivashankar, Assistant Commissioner, Custom office, Jogbani, India

101. Rajiv Rausan, SDO, Pharbesganj, Forbesganj, India

102. Barun Mishra, Local Correspondent, Hindustan, Station Road, Jogbani, India, 8092687356

103. Ishworchandra Yadav, Local Correspondent, Dainik Jagaran, Mira Medical Hall, Jogbani, India

104. Debendra K. Subba, DIG, Armed Police Force, Eastern Division Office, Sunsari 9852055607

105. Gyanmani Paudel, Inspector, Armed Police Force, Eastern Division Office, Sunsari

106. Madhab Ghimire, Regional Correspondent, Kantipur, Biratnagar, 9852029888

107. Vinod Bhattarai, Kantipur, , Biratnagar Office

108. Naraj Sahi, SSP Police, 9852000555

109. Taranath Gautam, CDO, Morong 9852057777

110. S.N. Harijan, ASI, Materuwa, Morang

111. Avinash Bohra, Morang Byapar Sangh, 9852020107

112. Mohammad Thule, Local, Koshi Barrage, Nepal

113. Ali Khan, Local, Koshi Barrage, India

114. Amit Tiwari, Custom officer, Sunsari Custom, 9852030559

115. Ramesh Prasad, Superintendent, Bihar Police, Sursand, India

116. Bashistha Yadav, Immigration Officer (SI), Sursand, India

117. Birendra Pandey, member of Bhansar Agent Sangh, Bhittamod , Nepal 9854030966

118. Subarna Thapa Magar, SP, APF (Border Security Office) Janakpur, Nepal 9841274969

119. Ramasis Yadav, President of Federation of Nepalese Journalist, Dhanusha 9844020059

120. Rajesh Kumar Karna, Gen. Secretary, Indo-Nepal Cross Border Journalist Association

121. Sujeet K. Jha, Avenues TV/ Editor of www.mithila.com

122. Ashok Kumar Temani, Immediate past President, Birjanj Chamber of Commerce and Industries

123. Ganesh Prasad Loth, Past President, Birjanj Chamber of Commerce and Industries

APPENDICES

124. Pradeep Dedia, Vice President, Birjanj Chamber of Commerce and Industries

125. Prem Raj Pokhrel, SP, APF (Border Security Office) Birganj, Nepal 9851082823

126. R.B. Karki, DSP, APF (Border Security Office) Birganj, Nepal

127. Sanjay Kumar Das, Local inhabitant, Birganj, Nepal

128. Dhanesh Shah, Local inhabitant, Alau VDC, Parsa, Nepal

129. Hakim Miya, Local inhabitant, Alau VDC, Parsa, Nepal

130. Yogendra P. Mali, Local inhabitant, Alau VDC, Parsa, Nepal

131. Subhit Kumar Sunuwarm Immigration officer, Birganj, Nepal

132. Ms. Sangita Puri, Program co-ordinator, Maiti Nepal, Birgunj Branch Office

133. Ram Kanhaiya of Aulo, Birgunj

134. Uday Rana, Custom Officer, Birganj 9849690921

135. Sushil Paudel, Sub-Inspector of Armed Police Force (APF), Raxaul, Nepal

136. Munni Ram, Currency Broker, Raxaul, India

137. Rajeev Kurmi, Businessmen, Raxauk, India

138. Anand Singh, Head Constable, SSB-India, Raxaul, India

139. Udaya Raj Neupane, Inspector, APF Outpost, Gaur 9849498772

140. W. Yaima Singh, Assistant Commander, SSB, Bairgania Outpost. India, 9431821401

141. Jagdish Baitha, former School Teacher, Rautahat, Nepal

142. Dinesh Shrma, Local Entrepreneur of Steels, Bairgania, India

143. Bishwanath Prasad, Local inhabitant, Bairgania, India

144. Bharat Adhikari, SI, Nepal Police, Kacharwa, Bara, Nepal

145. Bindeshor Yadav, Local, Kacharwa, India

146. Dinesh Prasad Yadav, Kacharwa, Bara, Nepal

147. Shambhu Prasad Shah, businessman, (UML cadre)

148. Karna Chhetri, SI, Sushta Police Post, Nawalparasi, 9846261167

149. Gopal Gurung, Save Sushta Aviyan, Nawalparasi, 9747085220

150. Krishna Sharma, local inhabitant, Sushta, Nawalparasi 9857041748

151. Shiyaram Chaudhari, Inspector, APF, Belaspur Seema Suraksha Base, Sushta, Nawalparasi 9747044186

152. Chitra Bahadur Khatri, Security Base, Sushta

153. R P Upadhyay, Journalist, Tribeni,

154. Nabir Ghosi, SSB Constable, Chakdawa, West Champaran, India

155. Prakash B. Shah, DSP, APF Seema Suraksha Karyalaya, Belaspur, Nawalparasi

156. Chhedup Sherpa, SI, SSB-India Krishnanagar, India

157. Udaya Shrivastav 'Rajan', local correspondent, Hindustan, Krishnanagar, India

158. Bhojraj Parajuli Sharma, Constable, Indian Custom

159. Janaki Chaudhari, KI Nepal, Krishna Nagar

160. Narad Gautam, Chief Custom Officer, Krishna Nagar, 9841203643

161. Karna Bahadur Budha Magar, DSP, APF, Krishnanagar Outpost, 9801600711

162. Ishowri Pun, Inspector, APF Seema Suraksha Karyalaya, Kapilbastu

163. Raja Murad Ali, SI, SSB-India, Sunauli

164. P. Chakma, Assistant Commander, SSB-India, Sunauli, Maharajgenj, 91-7309477075

165. Chandrabhan Jaiswal, Vice Chairperson, Udhyog Byapar

APPENDICES

Mandal, Sunauli, India

166. Manoj Kumar Jaiswal, Nepali citizen/business person in Sunauli, India 9847022711

167. G. K Gupta, Assistant Immigration Officer, Sunauli India

168. Madhab Dhungana- Journalist, Bhairahawa, Rupandehi, 9857021590

169. Chetan Panta-Journalist, Bhairahawa, Rupandehi, 98570 20250

170. Bishnu Sharma, Bhairahawa, Rupandehi, 9857020242

171. T.P. Bhusal, Bureau Chief, Sidhartha FM/ Joint Secretary FNJ Rupandehi

172. Balkrishna Panthi, CDO, Rupandehi, 9857077777

173. Birendra Bahadur Air, DSP, APF, Seema Suraksha Karyalaya, Rupandehi 9841500951

174. Ajit Maskey, Inspector, APF, Seema Suraksha Karyalaya, Rupandehi

175. Mingmar Lama, SSP, Nepal Police, Rupandehi

176. Hari B. Pal, SP, Nepal Police, Rupandehi 0951280222

177. Laxman Chand, Head, Anti-human Trafficking Office, Banbasa, India

178. Manoj Khatri, Banabasa Immigration Office, India

179. Mira Singh, Head Constable, Anti-human Trafficking Office, Banbasa, India

180. Chandra Shekhar Kanyal, SI, Uttarakhanda Police, Banbasa, India

181. Archana, Constable, Anti-human Trafficking Office,

182. John Lenthang, SI, SSB-Banbasa Outpost, India

183. Bir Bahadur Shrestha, SP, APF, Seema Suraksha Karyalaya, Kanchanpur 9854750244

184. Prem Dhoj Shaha, DSP, APF, Seema Suraksha Karyalaya, Kanchanpur 9849747238

185. Narendra Karki, Local, Mahendranagar-10, Nepal

186. J.D Lalman, Hawaldar, SSB Outpost, Tanakpur, India

187. Mohandeep Jyosi, local

188. Direndra Sinal, Station Manager, Se-Phoksundo FM, Kanchanpur.

189. Bhagwan Singh Thagunna, Nasu, Khalanga Custom, Dharchula

190. Dhauli Bhatta, ASI, Nepal Police, Khalanga, Dharchula

191. Ganesh Samanta, SI, Uttarakhanda Police, Jhulaghat

192. Lokendra Rai, Chief, Mahakali Custom Office, Baitadi

193. Dhan Singh Basal, SI, SSB-India, Dharchula.

194. Deepak Chand, Constable, Nepal Police, Khalanga, Dharchula

195. Mushaphir, Taxi Driver, Raxaul

196. Shankar Shrestha, Journalist, Malangawa

197. Ashutosh Agrawal, Consul General, Consulate General of India, Birganj

198. Khilram Rawat, local businessman, Kunauli

199. Min Bahadur Sunar, Police Constable, Nepal Police, Kunauli

Appendix II

List of the Border ports visited during fieldwork

1. Nepalganj-Rupaidiya
2. Guleria-Murtia
3. Jamunai-Balegau
4. Dhangadi-Gaurifanta
5. Kakarvitta-Phoolbari
6. Bhadrapur-Galgalia
7. Pashupati Nagar
8. Biratnagar-Jogbani
9. Koshi Barrage-Bhim Nagar
10. Bhittamod-Sursand (Sitamadi)
11. Birganj-Raxaul
12. Gaur-Bairgania
13. Bara-Kacharwa
14. Gandak-Sushta
15. Jhulanipur (Nichlaul)
16. Belaspur-Thutibari
17. Krishnanagar
18. Sonauli-Belahiya

19. Mahendranagar-Banbasa

20. Brahmadev-Tanakpur

21. Khalanga –Dharchula

22. Jhulaghat-Baitadi

23. Thori-Bhiknathori

24. Inarawa-janaki Tola

25. Sonbarsa- Malangawa

26. Basbhitta-Balara

27. Majorganj- Gulariyatol (Nankar)

28. Arnah-Sijuwa

29. Pipraun-Lagma (Jatahi)

30. Duhabi (Dhanusa),

31. Janki Nagar-

32. Jai Nagar-Baldiha

33. Siraha-Betauna

34. Madar-Kamalabari

35. Tilathi-Rajbiraj

36. Rampura-Kunauli

Appendix III

Model Interviews

Group discussion with Pradhan of Gaun Shava (Rupaedia), Secretary Samsuddin Khan and others

We are facing problem of light. Borders are open. We have unlimited infrastructures here like transport facilities to central states of India through train and buses. We have three universities and other degree colleges here in border areas. The security forces, despite being aware of the smuggling and criminal activities, pretend as if everything is all right.

Absence of light in the border has allowed smugglers to carry illegal goods or restricted good as per Nepal-India agreement. Even the security agencies, who are supposed to regulate these anti-smuggling activities, are experiencing difficulty in reducing the problem.

Question: "If you see the infrastructure of Indian border area, it's even worse than Nepal's. What are the reasons behind such backwardness?"Regarding the Bihar and Uttar Pradesh states borders, What are your views as a local leader?"

Answer: the central government allocates budget for development equally to all states. UP is the largest state with 18 crore population, while it receives equal budget as any other small states like Tamil Nadu and Kerala.

The reason behind such backwardness can be attributed to the elected local leader and his /her party. In this area, Congress party represents, while the state government is led by the Socialist party. I think the border infrastructure problem will be partly resolved if the local elected leader or people's representative and government belong to same party.

Question: What about the union fund that directly reaches the gram/village?

Answer: We receive nearly Rs 10 Lakh for one Gram panchayat.

One gram panchayat usually has 3-4 thousand population but here in border area, with 10 lakh rupees we have to support around 12 thousand population and even more. In fact our panchayat should receive budget equal to that of Nagar panchayat or municipality.

Question: What do you think how government should plan the expenditure of budget of border development fund?

Answer: First the proposal and budget expenditure plan for border development should be asked from gram panchayat. For example, in our case of Rupaidiya, border fund should be spent more on Rupaidiya and its vicinity. The infrastructural expenditure should spread gradually. But in reality, budget is spent directly 10 km away from Rupaidiya and it is, for example Nanpara, far from the the main border area.

Border development fund is in full control of central development officers and we have no representatives. We have no role in the decision making of spending border fund. I think If the fund for border development is deposited in our local development fund (where we have direct access) then the border area would be fantastically developed.. There is a huge amount of money in border development. In my view it is more than Rs 10 crore in total.

Question: There is an open border system here. What do you think about Nepal-India border relation and where is it heading ?

Answer: We have open border but there is no proper supervision or monitoring of the goods that pass through the states. Consumer goods brought by both the Nepalese and Indians from states Need to cross many check points. But goods illegally brought by the smugglers find their way into Nepal and India. Such smuggling business should be strictly monitored in order to discourage the illegal trade.

Question: In your views how reforms can be made in outpost border area and the passage of goods between India-Nepal?

Answer: I think there should be extra check-posts installed at the distance of two and half or three kilometer distance so that goods could pass only after the check by the security agencies.

Question: What is your assessment of SSB ?

Appendices

Answer: SSB of core border area or Zero km area whose activity can be seen are fine but problems are created by those staying far in the outposts.

Question: Do you know we have another problem or issue of Indo-Nepal border. Many talk about double citizenship. Do you know anything about that?

Answer: From our government perspective, double citizenship is undoubtedly wrong and illegal. When I talk from my personal experience, I think double citizenship is a kind of compulsion created by the border context rather than attempt to break the law or create any problems from others. I have seen people expanding families in both areas of Nepal and India border and peoples dwell on a regular basis.

Also, these double citizenship issues should be checked because people are talking about double advantages. We have seen that having Nepalese and Indian citizenship has allowed one to buy food in subsidy facilitated by Indian government while on the other side Indian people by making Nepalese passport have gone to gulf countries. There are other implications also created by double citizenship.

Question: How would you see the closure of Indo-Nepal border?

Answer: This would be problematic if border is closed because there is already high dependency among people living in the border area. Labor demand in Indian border side is high and Nepalese have got employment opportunities there through which they support their livelihood. People enjoy the same types of festivals, cultural activities and marriage relationship. Living and business have also made hem dependent. . All the construction activities in Nanpra area of India which is 10km distance from Rupaidiya, are dependent on labor force from Nepalgunj. Family members are expanded over all border area.

Hence, border shouldn't be closed but the monitoring level should be raised to control illegal and smuggling activities by improving the security.

SSB 6, 7 and 8 Battalion since they came here in 2003 haven't been changed.. For this long period of 10 years, SSB officials especially lower level to higher have established relations with smugglers and found many underground sources of income.

Question: What is the real problem with the border at general citizen level?

Answer: Dual citizenship is a compulsion for people living along the border. People residing over 10 km far from the border won't make dual citizenship because they don't need. But the border area people spreading over 1-2 km have half family in Nepali side and remaining half on the Indian side through which they have to commute .So they opt for dual citizenship.

Any idea of closure of border will trigger off migration of peoples; stop the source of revenue for country and source of income from citizen of both countries.

Question: What difference do you see in the situation of border area before and after SSB arrived in 2003?

Answer: Before SSB arrived in 2003, there used to be a huge number of robbery from Nepalese border village Kalabanjar and Mansipurva. They used to come in full-truck or trolley from Nepal at night in Rupaidiya, and rob the villages, murder Indian people and create terror among Indian border villages. But since 2003 when SSB arrived no such incident has occurred (except one a month ago). This total control over open robbery at night time is the greatest achievement of SSB

Question: What is the degree of control over smuggling by the SSB's presence in the border?

Answer: It's important to note that for 2-3 years, after SSB arrived in 2003, people hardly dared to do smuggling. They used to perceive SSB as strict military forces and were afraid of getting sever punishments or killed after being caught red hand by them. But slowly as the public relation and brotherhood feeling developed between SSB and local people , increase in smuggling was noticed.

Question: Do you think SSB would do its proper duty if it tries to keep a distance from the public?

Answer: yeah .it is to be noted that the SSB higher officers are not corrupt. The lower level SSB officers and staffs mobilized in the gate post and other entry points allow smugglers to enter because they already have underground links with them.

The major smuggling occurs on fertilizers because the subsidy given by the Indian government reduces the price. SSB should stop this but hasn't been able to do it.

Question: Let's talk about other probable border problems. As we see there are taxi standing in the Indian border to take passengers to Lucknow. Nepalese passengers who want to go for medical check up in Lucknow complains of not being treated properly and they were not taken to destinations in time despite taking more money. They complain that even after sitting in taxi and paying fare already, the vehicle don't head towards destination for at least one hour. Can you manage this?

Answer: They can be managed well. There is one taxi stand which runs on rotation basis by following rules. Fair is fixed at Rs 300 for Lucknow from fixed taxi stand. Other taxis standing there will also take the same amount.

There are other problems faced by Nepalese people in the Indian border. Nepalese labor migrants returning to Nepal are harassed in the border making them pay some amount by the officers at check post. Custom officers (Not SSB) take small amount of money from them. But these problems are not discussed publicly and no complaints have been filed.

SSB officials allow Nepalese people pass their daily consumption goods from India to Nepal on the humanitarian basis. Though some money might be asked by SSB at India Border, there are more problems at Nepal border. Nepal Police have made the border people suffer more while passing their goods in and out of the check post.

We don't have problems if Nepalese come to Indian-Border-Rupahidiya and buy their goods and talk back to their home. But these people suffer more in Nepalese border in comparison with the Indian side.

Indian four wheelers, 10 wheelers, when found committing small mistake in Nepalese road are harassed, exploited and physically assaulted by Nepalese traffic police officers and local people. They are charged money unnecessarily. Suppose if an Indian plate number vehicle running ion Nepalese road touches a Nepalese vehicle, the reaction from Nepalese side is violent. What we often hear is -10-12 local people gather and torture the vehicle staffs inhumanly, while if same incident occurs in India, we show sympathy and manage the problem without too much loss to Nepalese people. It is to be noted that general citizen of India are liberal and positive towards Nepali. But why is that? We think that Nepalese buyers are our customers, source of income and livelihood for us. So Indian businessman and vendors behave approximately with Nepalese people but if an Indian do a business in Nepalese border area and makes some mistake, then 10-12 people gather and torture heavily.

And we have seen problem in Nepalese government also in dealing with border issues. There are so many vehicles (motor cycles, car, and jeep) that enter Nepal illegally. We have heard that Nepal government doesn't show strictness for controlling such illegal business.

We had a person named Zamim who entered Nepal with a Mahindra Jeep. After Bhalubang of Dang district of Nepal, nobody knew our movement and also about the. It shows the deplorable security situation.

In India, we are liberal because we believe in give and take attitude towards Nepalese people. We also expect same in Nepal. In Nepal, so many police officials and leaders use four wheelers, bought from India illegally.

Question: Is it said that Nepalese women who cross into India from Nepal are investigated by the SSB's male security person in India. Is it so?

No, it is a lie which is circulated to do harm to the reputation of SSB. We have female police here in all the check posts, since three years, to search females crossing to India.

What was the case three years ago?

Since we didn't have female police in our post, less Nepalese women were caught as *charesh smugglers*. But after deploying women police and searching thoroughly, almost 200 Nepalese women have been caught transporting *charesh*. They are now in Bahirahi jail. The rise in number is because of women police deployed by the SSB, and thorough searching conducted b y them on the border.

Question: Why do you think women are being caught in charehs smuggling?

APPENDICES

Answer: Much women were caught carrying the Charesh across the border after the induction of SSB women personnel.

We request Nepal government to solve this issue of high involvement of women in *charus* smuggling, because all these women who are caught with *charus* are only carriers and are paid 1000, 2000 or 5000 for smuggling *charus* from Nepal to India. These women are being put into jail for long period of time and thus are being victimized. Nepal government should think about it.

Question: Some people blame SSB for this. They say, SSB in order to show their performance create false smugglers of drug entering from Nepal to India and arrest them.

Answer: These are all done to harm the reputation of SSB. Because, women who have been arrested till now have given statement to print and to the electronic media claiming that certain persons have given them money for smuggling drug across border. These women are still in jail; you can go and talk to them where they will explain you where they were given drug and to whom they have been asked to pass the *charus*. So, all the women who have been caught are real drug carrier. Also, there are few children in the group who have been used by the gang and are caught.

Question: Who are the people using Nepalese women for drug smuggling?

Answer: They are people from Nepal, Nepalese. These are professional people. But, yes, the women who are used as carrier are poor and illiterate..

Question: Do you think that these women, used as carrier, know that they are smuggling drugs?

Answer:

- No, many people don't know that they are carrying drugs with them from Nepal to India. I was talking with women used as carrier, as a press reporter, where they explained that they don't know the person who gives drugs to them. They are only asked to transport the drug to Rupaedia and get few thousands rupees. This explanation has been put forward dozens of time. These women are caught in border by SSB while they are entering India and sometimes they are caught when they do not find the person to pass the drug in Rupaedia and return to Nepal.

- Poverty and illiteracy are the main reasons behind women being used as drug smugglers. Nepal government should pass their attention to these issues as well.

- Nepal government is silent over the issue. From India's side, we are trying to control the drug smuggling. Subash Chandra Sharma, once a DM of this area, had submitted a list of 120 women involved in drug smuggling and are now jailed in India but Nepal government is mum over the issue. They have not even discussed the issue in the meeting held between India and Nepal every six month. This issue is already four year old and was explained to Nepalese side in Rupaedia Guest House.

- Many Nepalese women are now in Bahirahi jail now. The number has increased from 120 to 200. Every woman will be given more than 10 years of imprisonment by the court because each of them has been arrested with more than 4-5 kilos of *charus*. SSB has already arrested 50 quintals of *charus* till now.

Question: Is it only charus or other kinds of drug too ?

Answer:

- It is mostly *charus*. But yes, sometimes cocaine, smack and opium have also been caught.

- I have contacted few people from Dang and Surkhet and talked as a reporter. Their contact numbers were given to me by a woman carrier caught here (Rupaedia) saying that the persons carrying the number were her relative. I have talked to them where they explained that the woman caught is a distant relative and have also accepted that they have given the drug to her. Then I requested them to come to India to see her but no one has turned up. This is just a month -old case.

- But you have to understand one thing. These women know what they are carrying with them. It is because these carriers are asked to wear special dress. So they know what they are carrying or at

APPENDICES

least they can guess it is something unusual which they have been asked to transport. So, everyone knows about it. But because of poverty and the money they can earn, they still do the job.

Question: What are the main problems of this area?

Answer:

- The main problem of this area is that the train line in operation here is meter gauge if the line is converted into broad gauge. , all the businessmen from both Nepal and India will be benefited.

- Besides, transportation will also be easier for people. For example, at present people have to do reservation from Gonda to go big cities like Delhi, Lucknow;. if broad gauge line is constructed , reservation can be done from Rupaedia itself. We want to see trains leaving for Delhi and Lucknow from here (Rupedia) itself. At present, one has to go to Gonda and then to Lucknow where they can catch the main trains.

- Before the line is converted into a big one, we want to increase the number of trains coming to this area which will ultimately help in growth of business.

- But, Nepalganj Road Railway Station has been neglected because the work for broad gauge has already started from Krishnanagar to Gonda leaving Rupaedia.

Question: With increase in transportation facilities, will not the crime increase in this area ?

There are agencies to look after crimes. And, at present, this place is almost crimeless. There are no crimes like murdering and kidnapping. Yes, there are some crimes committed only to manage hand-to-mouth problem, which can be handled locally.

Question: You told that this place do business of million Rupees each day. Do the businessmen pay tax locally?

Answer:

- No, we are not paid the tax. Before we used to collect tax but now stay order has been released by the court. But yes, district council collects the tax from the businessmen.

- We are just given 1-2 million rupees through which we are developing the place. But we are in a process to declare this place as a town so that we can collect tax locally for local activities.

Question: What are the things that should be done for the development and benefit of this area including Nepal?

Answer:

- In the first place, this area should be declared a town from Gaun Shava. We meet the requirements of 20 thousand populations, a degree college, etc and for a Gaun Shava to be declared a mini-town. We have all the infrastructure and facilities in this place which needed a place to declare a mini-town. If this place is declared a town, then we will receive 10 million rupees yearly in addition to taxes which we can collect locally.

- This will also help us to build a parking place for vehicles without which a lot of problems, even for pedestrians, is already visible.

- This place if changed into town will help both India and Nepal. In addition, this will also help us improve the image of India in Nepal.

- Moreover, the dry port to be built in Rupedia (as in Birjung) will help regulate the traffic and other law and order issues of the area. This will also help control the problem of smuggling. The one-point barrier will solve many such issues, but the pilot project in Rupedia has been delayed from Indian side. We don't have any information about the progress. Incase of Nepal, construction of dry port is one the way and the progress seems satisfactory.

Appendices

Birendra Bahadur Rawal (Editor, Morning Bell), Naresh Pandey, Government Official, Dhangadi, Kailali

Question: What is going with the open border? What are the necessary reforms according to your local experience?

Answer: When we talk about the security and development situation in the border area, we have to talk about why crimes occur in the border area frequently and why huge number of security officials are mobilized and put on alert in border. The presence of professional criminals is due to the extreme poverty which is rampant in the border area.

During Maoist war (1996-2005), , I can remember there used to be exchange of guns and explosive materials between Maoist of Nepal and professional criminals groups of India through border.

Poverty is so worse that a poor youth border could kill anyone for money. Suppose one has to receive Rs 10 lakhs from a business man or any other, then professional killers were/are hired for money at the cost of someone's life.

Bribery and illegal smuggling is rampant in the small check post of Border. Such crime and illegal activities occur under political support and backup.

Nepal police, NGO workers and Indian police have worked together to stop the criminal activities in the border area but sometimes such criminal activities becomes difficult to handle. Nepalese criminals enter Indian border and Indian criminals enter Nepalese border. In recent one month 6-7 cases of loot, abductions were reported in Kailali.border areas.

The terror activities happen in border area under political protection. Though there hasn't been any recent big gun firing or violent incident but 6-7 incidents have already been seen where Nepal police, NGO workers confronted the professional criminals loaded with guns.

The issue of encroachment of GaiheraTaal (Deep Lake) was in light sometimes ago in Nepal-border area. Since 2040 B.S, Nepalese people were using that lake for fishing, and used the revenue of selling fish to run the local school. The fishing business was given on a contract to local people. After sometimes, 3-4 years back from now, SSB, local leaders and cadres went there in school area, removed the border pillar and chased away the Nepalese from there. This incident got much attention of both the people and the media. Such incident occurs in other areas as well.

I think such border conflicts could have been solved through the table talk by SSB, border security staffs, local leaders and student leaders, but in that particular case of Lake -Indian officials dominated the situation and took it on their side.

Conflict in border area should be taken as a common phenomenon. SSB removed the pillar in the border side belonging to Nepal and nobody has been informed regarding the whereabouts of the local people. Did they migrate elsewhere after the incident?.

There is a *Hulaki marga* (Highway) being constructed along Nepal and India border by India. There was protest by the locals against the road construction because the construction was going to create flooding problem for them. Local people residing in these places haven't experienced flooding before. After the road construction, they fear, of flooding to be caused by water logging.

Looting and robbery is common in Tikapur area. Since the arrival of CBI, cold relation is observed.

We are too much annoyed by the SSB officials especially by the lower level officials. Higher SSB officers don't bother to charge any money unnecessarily or illegally. If you see in the border gate post areas, daily wage workers who have to pass through border for their livelihood, have to pay Rs 200 to Rs 400 and sometimes mobiles are confiscated. It is like the violation of human rights.

Question: I heard that there is group or network of rickshaw pullers consisting of 25-30. Don't they allow people to come here? Is that true?

Answers: yes Sir, there is a network of 60-70 rickshaw owners in Indian border who only target lahures (soldiers) returning to Nepal. Even police have internal give-take with that network.

It's been one and half months, there was an incident of rape in the border jungle by one of the rickshaw owners belong to the same network. The Nepalese girl belonged to '*Mukta Kamaiya*' (freed bonded worker).

APPENDICES

That network has direct hand in that incident.

When we talk about traits of police, then everyone knows how rudely they behave with local people and returning migrants while passing through border gate posts. They threaten the vendors, cycle riders carrying sacks and bags or even Thela (four wheeler rickshaw) to open the sacks or pay Rs 500. Those border police men even check if they have mobile and confiscate it if their demands were not fulfilled.

Question: What about the treatment of police officials of Nepal border to the daily workers who pass by?

Answer: Nepalese security officers at Nepalese border have also imitated the same threatening behavior of Indian counterparts.

Question: Haven't media reported about such wrong –irresponsible activity of Nepalese police officials?

Answer: Rickshaw owners are mostly Nepalese. We have informed about such activity of Rickshaw owner to police. Police stopped such activity for four weeks but rickshaw owner organized road strike and did *chakka* jam. These things are even clear and you can know through anyone in Rupaediya.

There was incident when the smuggler physically attacked the custom office and emptied the check post. They didn't allow officers to stay in check post.

The reality in border is that since it is high earning spot for both Indian and Nepalese custom officers and security staffs, everyone is pre-determined to charge money from those who cross the border and earn money caring little about right or wrong.

Influence of Muslim community is also noticed in the border area. Earlier there was terror and fear of Alkaida or Laden terrorist group. Even some local Chaudharis living in the border area annoyed us too much. But they were caught by the police.

In the Far Western region, drug trafficking is common as the carriers are also from Rukum, Rolpa and Salyan districts.

Talking about weapon ownership in border area, there is no single house where people haven't owned weapon of one or other kind. Each house has at least one sharp knife (Kattari / Khukuri) and they are illegally kept. From India, illegal guns are smuggled in to Nepal and from Nepal side, drugs are supplied to India.

Talking about Nepalese border area, we have seen that since the time of king Mahendra, there is an area called Purnabaas, phoolbaari which is heavily dominated by ex-army or retired Indian *lahures*. In these areas the incident of loot and robbery hasn't occurred. But the cases of murder and robbery are increasing day by day especially in the jungle area of border.

We talked about the development situation in the border area as you know poverty is pervasive here.

Question: Now let's talk about positive side of the border area.

Answer: Employment opportunity is the most visible positive side. 30-40% people of Nepal border area- most of whom even belong to *Mukta Kamaiya* are working in Indian streets and building construction sites. Open border has facilitated big space for employment.

May daily food items are bought from Indian border market at lower price (than in Nepal).

There was even an effort from a local in Indian border area for fencing or construction of 7 fe et. When asked about the reason behind that, a local sardar said that since there was too much girls-trafficking incidents taking place from Nepal, it was built to stop such activities so that their area would have no relation with India and Nepal.

One case of minor man-handling was reported when one SSB had come to Nepalese area . Before that once an SSB had shot dead a woman in Custom office area. Bandha (strike) was organized for two-three days. Even Nepalese security can't do anything about such incidents..

Once there a pillar was found in the No-man's land area. In the evening, at 6 O'clock, a phone call came from Indian side for removing the pillar. Immediately we went there along with journalist, NGO workers, and security officers in the area where those unknown people were digging out the pillar. They could have removed it next morning if we would not have reached there in time. Later when we reached there they escaped

APPENDICES

from there. However, this issue was settled after consultation and after that they apologized to us. Once there was a row over the issue of burning dead bodies on the bank of the river, generally used by both the Indians and Nepalese for that purpose. Since the river changes it course, such disputes often arise.

Compared to Nepalgunj and other places of Nepal, the border in the Far Western Region is quiet.

Reaction from Nepal side came in response to baseless statements of local Indian leaders, High security officials of Indian border side. Till now there hasn't been any official claim of Indian government over Nepalese border area or land.

During the period of political instability or regime change, the issue of border encroachment arise.

Nepalese criminals operate with the help of Indian accomplices but the Indians themselves have not found committing crimes inside Nepal by themselves.

Stealing vehicles from India and selling them in Nepal is still a common phenomenon. It's very difficult to find who stole from where, and who sold to whom. Sometimes, fake number plates of vehicles are used along the border areas.

Question: What is size of users of this border?

Answer: People of Dadeldhura, Baitadi, Darchula, Kailali and other districts (6 districts in total) usually pass from here in huge numbers. On daily basis, more than 1000 people go to India. In season even 10,000 people cross the border everyday.

Dhangadi has become the central point for smuggling and other kinds of illegal trade.

Question: Why Bangladeshi and Pakistani also use this border?

Answer: it's very difficult to differentiate Pakistani and Indian. Pakistani people look like Muslim and have relations with Muslims of Dhangadhi. Most of the Mothersa (Muslim school) exist in Dhangadi and those Pakistani come here in the name of culture and religious education and fulfill their hidden agendas.

People work in Delhi as the Indian capital is near from the border. The security condition in border area is obviously not so good but technical authorities of both countries can sit together and solve the problem. Security condition is disturbed only when criminal act starts either from Nepalese or Indian side..

Question: what to improve the situation?

Answer: There are 2-3 things to consider. Number 1 is security inefficiency in border. I think SSB alone is insufficient to manage the security issues. There should be other mechanisms to improve security and enhance efficiency.

Number 2: There should be an independent body or authority to monitor SSB activities in the border area. You can't imagine how corrupt they are. Suppose you are smuggling something from India to Nepal, then you can pass it without check in just Rs 2000.

Question: Do the SSB personnel take money to allow the smuggled goods?

Answer: yes, they are SSB staffs. We have (Journalists) even live photos showing SSB with money in hand before allowing the passage of goods in border. Nowadays we have observed such roles of Nepali APF also.

Recently we are doing investigation over how criminal's carryout abduction and other illegal activities by using n-cell mobile in No-man's land area. It has both benefits and drawbacks as well.

There are two lines of authorities in Nepalese border area. There is conflict of interest between SP and DSP. SP doesn't want to take bribe while DSP is corrupted and don't do anything without money.

Nepal APF, SSP carry out all of these smuggling activities in the border. But DSP tryies to stop and creates obstacles in the smuggling activities allowed by SSP.

You can image if Army or SSP level officers are engaged in illegal activities then what kind of security we expect in border area?

APPENDICES

Question: What will be the last solution in Nepal?

Answer: In Nepal, Poverty is the root problem that triggers security problem in border. So poverty alleviation programs should be carried out actively.

Another problem is the dependency of Nepalese police administration and Nepal government on India. Even for small things and issue we Nepalese seek help from others. So we should enhance our own production mechanism.

Import of Onion and Chillies, Garlic and other vegetable items from India through fully loaded trucks used to take place before. But now people of Nepalese border take benefit of open border and work in Indian border to sustain their livelihood. So employment if guaranteed for the poor people living in border area, there will be much progress in security situation.

As we see, SSB and Border security officer are active only during day time. And during night, criminals are active. Security to control them should be devised. Another important issue to consider is the legal action against those criminals.

And we also clarify that arranging Visa-passport system is not appropriate in Nepal India –open border.

Nepal should monitor activities of Nepalese going out of the country.

Appendix IV

Detail of the unresolved spots and pockets of Nepal - India border

Number	District	Municipality/ VDC- Ward Number	Spots of disputes, conflicts and encroachment	Area in hectare (approximately)	Date (approx)
1	Darchula	Byas- 1 and 2	Kalapani-Limpiyadhura (encroached during India-China border war)	37,000	November 1962
2	Kanchanpur	Bhimdatta Municipality-9	Khalla Masita of western Brahmadevmandi and portion of Siddhanath temple	15	1972
3	Kanchanpur	Bhimdatta Municipality-10	West of Brahmadev Bazar (east of Tanakpur Barrage or area of submerged boundary pillar 2 and 3 and portion of Tanakpur afflux bund	222	December 1991
4	Kanchanpur	Bhimdatta Municipality- 11	The land to be obtained on the exchange of land, given by Nepal to construct the Sharada Barrage	15	1928
5	Kanchanpur	Bhimdatta Municipality- 11	Land from Banabasa embankment to the canal of Gadda Chauki	30	1979

APPENDICES

Number	District	Municipality/ VDC- Ward Number	Spots of disputes, conflicts and encroachment	Area in hectare (approximately)	Date (approx)
6	Kanchanpur	Rauteli Bichawa, Jhilimili	Various spots of Suklaphanta wildlife conservation area and near to missing boundary pillar (BP) number 229	330	2001
7	Kanchanpur	Rampur Bilaspur-1	Portion of Bhuda village, Patalchula Nala and portion of Pachue village	14	1978
8	Kanchanpur	Laxmipu-5	30 meter wide strip, south of Fatiya Gaon, near to BP-200	3	2007
9	Kanchanpur	Tribhuvanbasti-4	Kankadi Tal area near to the origin of Suheli Nala (Brook) i.e. land of Karna Bahadur Sunar, Nika Nepali and Man Bahadur Sunar	2	2007
10	Kanchanpur	Parasan-7, 8, 9	Pyara Tal (Nala) area (individual and government land from southern portion of Pyara Tal to fallen BP-195 and 6.6 hectare land belonged by Bichfanta National Secondary School)	980	1978, 2003, 2005 and 2006
11	Kailali	Fulbari-	Forest area cut by Indian (course changed by Mohana river area located south of Fulbari village)	5	2000

Number	District	Municipality/ VDC- Ward Number	Spots of disputes, conflicts and encroachment	Area in hectare (approximately)	Date (approx)
12	Kailali	Lalbojhi-8	Kauwakheda area (land of 25 families including Pratap Singh Saud)	212	2004
13	Kailali	Bhajani-9	Kusumghat area (land of 48 persons including Biru Bika)	39	3 January 2005
14	Bardiya	Rajapur-	South of Rajapur settlement area near to the eastern branch of Karnali River	10	21 august 2006
15	Bardiya	Bhimapur-	Disputed area regarding present and the then course of Nakuwa Nala (brook)	10	1983
16	Bardiya	Khairi Chandanpur-	South of Khairi village located near to the bank of Geruwa River	4	
17	Bardiya	Gulariya Municipality- 4, 9, 10	Chaugurji area in between old BP- 63 and 64; and the land east of Thapuwa	7	
18	Bankay	Holiya- 8, 9	Holiya area, located west of River Rapti and the land located north-west of BP- 19	42	2001
19	Bankay	Narainapur-	Kerbariya Nala area located south of Narayanpur and north-west of Ghordhoriya	9	2006

APPENDICES

Number	District	Municipality/ VDC- Ward Number	Spots of disputes, conflicts and encroachment	Area in hectare (approximately)	Date (approx)
20	Dang	Koilabas-2	Along the road from Koilabas Bazar to India and the land adjoined to BP- 39/600	25	1983
21	Kapilbastu	Krishnanagar-	Krishnanagar Bazar in the northern portion of No-man's land of BP- 67/1	1	
22	Rupandehi	Ajma-	Marchawar area (South of Ajma settlement and west of Dano River along BP- 30)	50	1999
23	Rupandehi	Siddhartha Nagar Municipality-	Belhiya border crossing area (Indians have constructed huts and houses along 10 meter wide strip)	5	
24	Nawalparasi	Susta- 1 to 4 and 6 to 9	As the river Narayani changed its course towards Nepal frontier, Indians have encroached the river left over area.	14,500	1845, 1941, 1954, 1964, 1975, 1986 and 2008
25	Chitawan	Rastriya Nikunja-	East of Tribenighat and south of Balmiki Ashram that Indians cut the forest and encroached the land	170	1979
26	Chitawan	Madi Kalyanpur-	Portion of Madichure along Dara Nala	4	

Nepal – India Open Border: Problems and Prospects

Number	District	Municipality/ VDC- Ward Number	Spots of disputes, conflicts and encroachment	Area in hectare (approximately)	Date (approx)
27	Parsa	Thori (Nayabasti)	Thute Khola, Thute Khola, South-east of Thori Bazar and Thori River and the area where BP- 64 was washed away by the river	70	1995, 2010
28	Parsa	Janaki Tola-9	Western part of Dasauta village (from BP- 419/20 to 420/13)	7	June 2009
29	Parsa	Mahadevpatti- 6	Laxmipur Pipra area (south of the road which leads to Jaya Mangalpur)	135	July 2009
30	Parsa	Birganj Municipality-	East of Customs office near to Ahir Tola and BP- 390 along Sirsiya River	10	
31	Parsa	Birganj Municipality-19	Chamar Tola of Inarwa near Miteri bridge (old Junge Pillar 33 to 35 were not recognized as main boundary pillar)	6	February 2002
32	Parsa	Birganj Municipality-6	Portion of the 27.71 Acres of land from Miteri Bridge to Prewo Tola, bought by Nepal Government Transport Corporation from India on 29 June 1924	5	1990
33	Bara	Dakchhin Jhitkaiya-6, 8	West of Katihariya and Fulbariya and east of Pasaha River adjoined with No-man's land of BP381/31	30	2003

Appendices

Number	District	Municipality/ VDC- Ward Number	Spots of disputes, conflicts and encroachment	Area in hectare (approximately)	Date (approx)
34	Rautahat	Jokaha-7	Southern portion of Jamuna Jayanagar village that Indians cut the forest trees	15	
35	Sarlahi	Tribhuvan Nagar-	Tribhuvan settlement area located east of Jhim River, 70 metre wide strip from BP- 25 to 35, 38 and 39	4	
36	Sarlahi	Narayanpur-	Portion of Sangrampur village located at west of Hardi River	8	1980
37	Mahottari	Samsi-	Portion of Kanawa Haat Bazar area. located west of Samsi Bazar area and east of BP- 313/3	5	
38	Mahottari	Siswa Kataiya-	West of Siswa Katiya settlement (original BP- 11 shifted to 50 metre north)	9	2001
39	Siraha	Madar-	Inarwa Tola of Madar and southern portion of Chandraganj (southern area of the road from Siraha Bazar to Indian frontier)	7	
40	Siraha	Inarwa-	Western portion of Thandi and Bhati Balan River (land along the road from Thandi village to India)	4	
41	Saptari	Deuri-	Suwarnapatti area (50 meter wide strip along the river Kharag, shifting the pillar to Nepal side)	40	

Number	District	Municipality/ VDC- Ward Number	Spots of disputes, conflicts and encroachment	Area in hectare (approximately)	Date (approx)
42	Saptari	Baniyani-	Bardahi village area, near to Bhutahidhar river	14	
43	Saptari	Chhinnamasta-3	Near to Balarampur, south of Sakhada Bhagawati temple	10	
44	Saptari	Lalapatti-	Govindapur area (shifted Junge BP 60 to 100 metre towards Nepal	33	
45	Saptari	Tilathi-	Kunauli area Nepal's government fallow land along the road from Kunauli to Nirmali Railway Station (demolished BP- 223/13)	40	
46	Saptari	Gobargadha-	Various spots from Bishnupur to Shivanagar area	8	
47	Saptari	Gobargadha-	Southern area of Gobargadha (west of River Koshi and south of Gobargadha)	30	
48	Sunsari	Hariharpur-9	Bhantabari-Kataiya (500 metre east of Koshi Barrage and south of East-West Highway, where there was a border wooden gate previously)	15	1982
49	Sunsari	Kaptanganj-	Portion of Shivaganj and Pakariya	8	
50	Sunsari	Sahebganj-	South of Sahebganj habitation and west of Katlaha River	20	

Appendices

Number	District	Municipality/ VDC- Ward Number	Spots of disputes, conflicts and encroachment	Area in hectare (approximately)	Date (approx)
51	Morang	Biratnagar Sub-metropolitan City- 20	Part of Budhnagar, near to industrial area of Rani Jogbani border	7	March 1999
52	Morang	Rangeli-	Wouka and Chopraha inhabitation near to the road to India from Rangeli Bazar	13	
53	Morang	Bardanga-	Part of Doriya located at east of Sonapur settlement and east of Bakraha (Luna) River	15	
54	Jhapa	Korobari-2, 4	Cultivated land of 33 families of Korobari area, shifting BP-140	41	
55	Jhapa	Pathamari-	Near to Pathamari village located west of River Mechi (Sub-Customs Office and some cultivated land)	10	
56	Jhapa	Maheshpur-2	Encroached east of Dol Gaun and India planned Indira Housing Project	10	March 2000
57	Jhapa	Bhadrapur Municipality-	Eastern portion of Bhadrapur School playground that leads to Galgaliya railway station of India (degraded the status of Junge main boundary pillar PP-1 to reference pillar)	27	1994

Number	District	Municipality/ VDC- Ward Number	Spots of disputes, conflicts and encroachment	Area in hectare (approximately)	Date (approx)
58	Jhapa	Jyamirgadhi- 1, 2	Kalikhajar area, lands of Jetha Rai, Pradip Karki, Ishwsori Rai have been encroached	10	12 November 2011
59	Jhapa	Mechinagar Municipality-11	Bhansa Khola (Upreti village) at Kankarbhitta area, located at the western bank of River Mechi and encroached 67 metre span of Mechi Bridge	41	December 2006
60	Jhapa	Mechinagar Municipality-	Nakalbanda area consisting of Madanjot and Warisjot, shifting the BP-46 to Nepal side	15	
61	Jhapa	Bahundangi-	Patapur of Tiring located north of Bahundangi habitation	20	1940
62	Ilam	Shree Antu-8	Gufapatal area encroached by Indian Forest Office and Chhabbise area encroached by Jawahar Nawodaya School of India	9	1981

Appendices

Number	District	Municipality/ VDC- Ward Number	Spots of disputes, conflicts and encroachment	Area in hectare (approximately)	Date (approx)
63	Ilam	Pashupatinagar-4, 5, 9	Phatak area encroached by Indian Customs and Police Post building; and 240 sq mtr vacant land. SSB 29th Battalion encroached Hile Penal area and Pul Khola area. India constructed graveyard and Buddhist Monastery near Simana Bazar of Nepal. Indians encroached Panch Mile area and also six homes of Nepali at Hile Bhaijyang, including government Sub-Customs Office	15	2004, 2008 and 2010
64	Ilam	Gorkhe-9	Manebhanjyang Simana Bazar area and foot trail-road of Gairibas area	4	2005
65	Ilam	Maimajuwa-	Sandakpur hill top and 12 kilometre strip of Meghma-Tumling-Kalpokhari area	54	
66	Panchthar	Prangbung- 6	Portion of Aahal Gairi area and Aahale Bhanjyang	14	2006
67	Panchthar	Chyangthapu-	Chiya Bhanjyang Singhalila range to Kabru and Talung. (Border line shifted to western side, ignoring the highest watershed, from Phalut to Kabru and Talung)	4,100	2003, 2004

Number	District	Municipality/ VDC- Ward Number	Spots of disputes, conflicts and encroachment	Area in hectare (approximately)	Date (approx)
68	Taplejung	Timbuk Pokhari-	Eastern hill of Timbuk Pokhari that encroached the watershed area by constructing Singhalila Park	400	
69	Taplejung	Kalikhola-	Eastern portion of the origin of river Kabeli Khola and Lamay Khola	800	
70	Taplejung	Yamphudin-	Eastern portion of Kabru area, taking the border as the lower watershed range	600	
71	Taplejung	Lelep	Part of Tumling habitation (the area east of Lelep and Yamphudin Village Development Committees	220	

Source: *http://bordernepal.wordpress.com/2013/05/*

Appendix V

TREATY OF SUGAULI, 2ND DECEMBER 1815 BETWEEN EAST INDIA COMPANY AND THE COUNTRY OF NEPAL

TREATY of PEACE between the HONOURABLE EAST INDIA COMPANY AND MAHA RAJAH BIRKRAM SAH, Rajah of Nepal, settled between LIEUTENANT – COLONEL BRADSHAW on the part of the HONOURABLE COMPANY, in virtue of the full powers vested in him by HIS EXCELLENCY the RIGHT HONOURABLE FRANCIS, EARL of MOIRA, KNIGHT of the MOST NOBLE ORDER of the GARTER, one of HIS MAJESTY's MOST HONOURABLE PRIVY COUNCIL, appointed by the Court of Directors of the said Honourable Company to direct and control all the affairs in the East Indies, and by SREE GOOROO GUJRAJ MISSER and CHUNDER SEEKUR OPEDEEA on the part of MAHA RAJAH GIRMAUN JODE BIKRAM SAH BAHAUDER, SHUMSHEER JUNG, in virtue of the powers to that effect vested in them by the said Rajah of Nepal, 2nd December 1815.

Whereas war has arisen between the Honourable East India Company and the Rajah of Nepal, and whereas the parties are mutually disposed to restore the relations of peace and amity which, previously to the occurrence of the late differences, had long subsisted between the two States, the following terms of peace have been agreed upon:

ARTICLE I

There shall be perpetual peace and friendship between the Honourable East India Company and the Rajah of Nepal.

ARTICLE II

The Rajah of Nepal renounces all claim to the lands which were the subject of discussion between the two States before the war, and acknowledges the right of the Honourable Company to the sovereignty of those lands.

ARTICLE III

The Rajah of Nepal hereby cedes to the Honourable the East India Company in perpetuity all the under-mentioned territories, viz-

First: – The whole of the low lands between the Rivers Kali and Rapti.

Secondly: – The whole of the low lands (with the exception of Bootwul Khass) lying between the Rapti and the Gunduck.

Third: The whole of the low lands between the Gunduck and Coosah, in which the authority of the British Government has been introduced, or is in actual course of introduction.

Fourth: All the low lands between the Rivers Mitchee and the Teestah.

Fifth: All the territories within the hills eastward of the River Mitchee including the fort and lands of Nagree and the Pass of Nagarcote leading from Morung into the hills, together with the territory lying between that pass and nagerr. The aforesaid territory shall be evacuated by the Gurkha troops within forty days form this date.

ARTICLE IV

With a view to indemnify the Chiefs and Barahdars of the State of Nepal, whose interests will suffer by the alienation of the lands ceded by the foregoing Article, the British Government agrees to settle pensions to the aggregate amount of two lakhs of rupees per annum on such Chiefs as may be selected by the Rajah of Nepal, and in the proportions which the Rajah may fix. As soon as the selection is made, Sunnuds shall be granted under the seal and signature of the Governor General for the pensions respectively.

ARTICLE V

The Rajah of Nepal renounces for himself, his heirs, and successors, all claim to or connextion with the countries lying to the west of the River Kali and engages never to have any concern with those countries or the inhabitants there of.

ARTICLE VI

The Rajah of Nepal engages never to molest to disturb the Rajah of Sikkim in the possession of his territories; but agrees, if any difference shall arise between the State of Nepal and the Rajah of Sikkim, or the subjects of either, that such differences shall be referred to the arbitration of the British Government by which award the Rajah of Nepal engages to abide.

ARTICLE VII

The Rajah of Nepal hereby engages never to take of retain in his service any British subject, nor the subject of any European or American State, without the consent of the British Government.

ARTICLE VIII

In order to secure and improve the relations of amity and peace hereby established between the two States, it is agreed that accredited Ministers from each shall reside at the Court of the other.

ARTICLE IX

This treaty, consisting of nine Articles, shall be ratified by the Rajah of Nepal within fifteen days from this date, and the ratification shall be delivered to Lieutenant-Colonel Bradshaw, who engages to obtain and deliver the ratification of the Governor-General within twenty days, or sooner, if practicable.

Done at Segowlee, on the 2nd day of December 1815.

PARIS BRADSHAW, Lt. Col., P.A.

Received this treaty from Chunder Seekur Opedeea, Agent on the part of the Rajah Nepal, in the valley of Muckwaunpoor, at half-past two o'clock p.m. on the 4th of March 1816, and delivered to him the Counterpart Treaty on behalf of the British Government.

D.D. OCHTERLONY,

Agent, Governor-General.

[Many words are not as per modern usage, they are written the same way as they were at that time]

Appendix VI

Nepal – Britain Friendship Treaty 21 December 1923

(**Treaty of Friendship between Great Britain and Nepal** signed at Kathmandu, 21st December 1923, and Note bearing the same date respecting the importation of Arms and Ammunition into Nepal – 1923) (Exchange of ratifications took place at Kathmandu on the 8th April 1925)

TREATY

Whereas space and friendship have now existed between the British Government and the Government of Nepal since the signing of the Treaty of Segowlie on the 2nd day of December 1815; and whereas since that date the Government of Nepal has ever displayed its true friendship for the British Government and the British Government has as constantly shown its good-will towards the Government of Nepal; and whereas the government of both the countries are now desirous of still further strengthening and cementing the good relations and friendship which have subsisted between them for more than a century; the two High Contracting Parties having resolved to conclude a new treaty of Friendship have agreed upon the following Article:-

Article I

There shall be perpetual peace and friendship between the Governments of Great Britain and Nepal, and the two Governments agree mutually acknowledge and respect each other's independence both internal and external.

Article II:

All previous treaties, agreements and engagements, since and including the Treaty of Segowlie of 1815, which have been concluded between the two Government are hereby conformed, except so far as they may be altered by the present Treaty.

Article III:

As the preservation of peace and friendly relations with the neighbouring States whose territories adjoin their common frontiers is to the mutual interests of both the High Contracting Parties, they hereby agree to inform each other of any rupture such friendly relations, and each to exert its good offices as far as may be possible to remove such friction and misunderstanding.

Article IV:

Each of the High Contracting Parties will use all such measure as it may deem practicable t prevent its territories being used for purpose inimical to the security of the other.

Article V:

In view of the long standing friendship that has subsisted between the British Government and the Government of Nepal and for the sake of cordial neighbourly relations between them , the British Government agrees that the Nepal Government shall be free to import from or through British India into Nepal whatever arms, ammunition, machinery, warlike material or stores may be required or desired for the strength and welfare of Nepal, and that this arrangement shall hold good for all times as long as the British Government is satisfied that the intentions of the Nepal Government are friendly and that there is no immediate danger to India from such importations. The Nepal such arms, ammunition, etc., across the frontier of Nepal either by the Nepal Government or by private individuals. If, however, any convention for the regulation of the Arms Traffic, to which the British Government may be a party, shall come into force, the right of importation of arms and ammunition by the Nepal Government shall be subject to the proviso that the Nepal Government shall first become a party to that Convention, and that such importation shall only be made in accordance with the provisions of that Convention.

Article VI:

No Customs duty shall be levied at British Indian ports on goods imported on behalf of the Nepal Government of immediate transport to that country provided that a certificate from such authority as may from time to time be determined by the two governments shall be presented at the time of importation to the Chief Customs Officer at the port of import setting forth that the goods are the property of the Nepal Government, are required for the public services of the Nepal Government are not for the purpose of any State monopoly or State trade, and are being to Nepal under orders of the Nepal Government, The British Government also agrees to the grant in respect of all trade goods, imported at British Indian ports for immediate transmission to Katmandu without breaking bulk en route, of a rebate of the full duty paid, provided that in accordance with arrangements already agreed to, between the two Governments, such goods may break bulk for repacking at the port of entry under Customs supervision in accordance with such rules as may from time to time be laid down in this behalf. The rebate may be claimed on the authority of a certificate signed by the said authority that the goods have arrive at Katmandu with Customs seals unbroken and otherwise untampered with.

Article VII:

This Treaty signed in the part of the British Government by Lieutenenat- Colonel W.F.T. O'Connor, C.I.E., C.V.O., British Envoy at the Court of Nepal and on the part of Nepal Government by General His Highness Maharaja Sir Chandra Shumsher Junga Bahadur Rana, G.C.B, G.C.S.I., G.D.M.G., G.C.V.O., D.C.I., Thong-lin Pimma Kokang- Wang-Syan, Prime Minister and Marshal of Nepal , shall be ratified and the ratification shall be exchanged at the Katmandu as soon as practicable.

Signed and sealed at Kathmandu this the twenty first day of December in the year one thousand nine hundred and twenty three Anno Domini Corresponding with the Sixth Paush, Sambat Era one thousand nine hundred and eighty.

(Under Vernacular Translation of Treaty)

W.F.T O'Connor,	Chandra Shumshere,
LT.Col.	Prime Minister and Marshal
British Envoy at the Court of Nepal	of Nepal.

Appendices

Note:- From the Prime Minister of Nepal, to the British Envoy at the Court of Nepal. December 21, 1923

My dear Colonel O'Connor, Regarding the purchase of arms and ammunitions which the Government of Nepal busy from time to time for the strength and welfare of Nepal, and imports to its own territory from and through British India in accordance with Article V of the Treaty between the two Governments, the Government of Nepal hereby agrees that it will, from time to time before the importation of arms and ammunition at British Indian Ports, furnish detailed lists of such arms and ammunitions to the British Envoy at the Court of Nepal in order that the British Government may be in a position to issue instructions to the port authorities to afford the necessary facilities for their importation in accordance with Article VI of this Treaty. I am, etc. Chandra

To
Lieutenant-Colonel W.F.T. O'Connor, C.I.E., CVO,
British Envoy at the Court of Nepal.

Appendix VII

MEMORANDUM OF BIPARTITE AGREEMENT BETWEEN THE GOVERNMENT OF THE DOMINION OF INDIA AND HM GOVERNMENT IN THE UNITED KINGDOM.

1. That all volunteers from Regular battalions of each of the Second, Sixth, Seventh and Tenth Gurkha Rifles, together with personnel of their Regimental Centres, shall be transferred to HM British Army, subject to the negotiation of terms and conditions with the Government of Nepal.

2. That the personal arms and equipment of those units if required by HM Government will be issued on payment, and removed overseas with the units.

3. That HM Government may for the present continue to use the existing recruiting depots at Gorakhpur and Ghum, and that the British and Gurkha military personnel serving in them may wear uniform.

4. That the plans of HM Government for recruiting in Nepal up to a possible strength of a Division (say 25,000 men) shall not in any way interfere with recruitment to the Gurkha units in the Indian Army.

5. That Gurkha Officers, recruits, soldiers, ex-soldiers and pensioners of Gurkha units serving HM Government, and their dependants, shall be permitted to travel freely between Nepal and an Indian port on their lawful occasions, provided mufti is worn in transit through India; the stipulation regarding dress shall not apply to the four Regiments named above during their removal from India.

6. That the normal road and rail transport facilities in India shall be available, at the public rates prevailing from time to time, to all British Officers serving with Gurkhas, Gurkha Officers and their

Appendices

families, Gurkha other ranks and their families and the necessary maintenance stores and baggage of such personnel in the service of HM Government; and that such staging facili- ties as may be required shall be provided at the expense of HM Government.

7. That India's postal, money order and telegraphic services to and from Nepal shall be available to HM Government, and Gurkhas serving HM Government, at the normal rates pre- scribed from time to time.

8. That the Government of India shall make available annually to HM Government, for the use of Gurkha soldiers, the following quantities of foodstuffs:-

Atta	2,200 tons
Ghee	750 tons
Dhal	1,200 tons
Condiment Powder	150 tons

provided HM Government arrange to supply the Government of India with 2,200 tons of wheat in replacement of the atta supplied to them.

9. That the Government of India shall make available to HM Government such Indian currency as may be necessary for purposes connected with their employment of Gurkha soldiers, provided that the sterling equivalent thereof shall be credited to the Government of India Sterling Account One.

10. That Gurkha Officers, soldiers, ex-soldiers, pensioners and their dependents shall have the right to send or take Indian money back to Nepal subject only to such Indian currency regulations of general application as may be in force from time to time; foreign currency imported into India shall be subject to the general Indian currency regulations obtaining from time to time.

11. That the basic rates of pay admissible to Gurkha Officers and soldiers serving HM Government shall approximate to those laid down in the present Indian Pay Code, at which rates personnel serving at the recruiting depots in Gorakhpur and Ghum shall be paid; and

that a special allowance, to compensate for permanent service overseas and high cost of living, shall in addition be admissible to Gurkha officers and soldiers serving HM Government overseas.

12. After the 8 Battalions have been asked to opt for service under HM Government, Government of India will try to make up the deficiency caused by those who do not wish to serve with HM Government, by asking other soldiers who have completed their existing engagement and who do not wish to continue to serve in the Indian Army units. If the required number cannot thus be made good the deficiency will be made up by HM Government by direct recruitment.

(Sgd) Kanwar Daya Singh Bedi (Lt. Col.)	(Sgd) A C B Symon
For the Government of the Dominion of India.	For His Majesty's Government in the United Kingdom.

Kathmandu

7th November, 1947.

NEPALESE OBSERVATIONS ON "POINTS OF AGREEMENT BETWEEN GOVERNMENT OF INDIA AND HMG".

Para (3) - It appears that the arrangement of having recruiting Depots at Gorakhpur and Ghum for the British Gurkha Regi- ments has as an after-thought been made of a temporary char- acter. Nepal Government feels that it would definitely be more convenient to all three parties, if the recruiting is carried on for both Indian and British Armies at the present depots or any other places in India.

Para (4) - In view of our long-standing friendship the Government of Nepal had agreed to raise the strength of the Gurkha Regiments during the period of the last war. But she feels that the continuation of this emergency measure will be too much of a drain on the man-power of the country. So she desires that the total be limited and brought down to the peace-time strength of 20 battalions to be divided between the Indian and British Armies, as already arranged.

Appendices

Para (10) - Nepal Government desires that the foreign currency brought by the personnel of the Gurkha Regiments serving abroad be credited to the Nepal Government account in any bank (to be settled afterwards) and Government of Nepal providing Indian Currency therefore at the prevailing market rate.

NEPALESE SUGGESTIONS TO HIS MAJESTY'S GOVERNMENT AND THE GOVERNMENT OF INDIA FOR THE EMPLOYMENT OF GURKHAS.

1. In all matters of promotion, welfare and other facilities the Gurkha troops should be treated on the same footing as the other units in the parent army so that the stigma of "mercenary troops" may for all time be wiped out. These troops should be treated as a link between two friendly countries.

2. The Gurkha troops should be given every facility so that it might be officered by their own men and they should be eligible to commissioned ranks with no restrictions whatsoever to the highest level to which qualified officers may be promoted.

3. The Gurkha troops should not be used against Hindu or any other unarmed mobs.

4. To avoid any clash between the Gurkhas themselves, Gurkha troops should not be used if any contingency of their having to serve in opposite camps arises.

5. To enable us to supply better quality men, we request that our following military needs may be met:-

    (i) A well-equipped arms and ammunition factory producing all modern small arms and ammunitions.

    (ii) A few Army transport planes.

    (iii) Our requirements of Army Stores and civil supplied could be discussed later on.

6. To establish better liaison between Nepal and the troops, liai-son officers would be appointed by the Nepalese Government and would form part of the unit of the Gurkha troops.

Appendices

7. It is very desirable that the morale of the recruits as well as the armed forces should remain unimpaired. Therefore all activities prejudicial to the interest and security of one party should be prevented in the territories of the other parties.

8. The Government of Nepal reserves the right to withdraw all Gurkha troops in case Nepal is involved in any war.

9. All facilities for the training of Nepalese officers in the military academies of India and Britain should be provided as and when the Nepal Government wants.

10. As Khukri is there religious and national emblem of the Gurkhas forming also a part of the uniform of the Gurkha Army, the carrying of Khukri by Gurkhas of all categories must not be banned in territories where the Gurkhas reside.

11. When Gurkha troops go on active service, intimation might be given to the Government of Nepal.

12. The above mentioned points are to be incorporated in a treaty and or agreement to be signed between the parties in due course.

Appendix VIII

Nepal – India Peace And Friendship Treaty

31 July 1950

The Government of India and the Government of Nepal recognizing the ancient ties which have happily existed between the two countries for centuries. Desiring still further to strengthen and develop these ties and to perpetuate peace between the two countries.

Have resolved therefore to enter into a treaty of Peace and Friendship with each other, and have, for this purpose, appointed as their plenipotentiaries the following persons, namely, the Government of India his Excellency Shri Chandreshwar Prasad Narain Singh, Ambassador of India in Nepal; The Government of Nepal, Mohan Shamsher Jang Bahadur Rana, Maharaja, Prime Minister and Supreme commander in Chief of Nepal, who having examined each other's credentials and found them good and in due form have agreed and follows:

Article I

There shall be everlasting peace and friendship between the Government of India and the Government of Nepal. The two Governments agree mutually to acknowledge and respect the complete sovereignty territorial integrity and independence of each other:

Article II

The two Governments hereby undertake to inform each other any serious friction or misunderstanding with any neighbouring State likely to cause any breach in the friendly relations subsisting between the two Governments.

Article III

In order to establish and maintain the relations referred to in Article I the two Governments agree to continue diplomatic relations with each other by means of representatives with such staff as is necessary for the due performance of their functions.

The representatives and such of these as may be agreed upon shall enjoy such diplomatic privileges and immunities as are customarily granted by International law on a reciprocal basis : Provided that in no case shall these be less than those granted to persons of a similar status of any other States having diplomatic relations with either Government.

Article IV

The two Government agree to appoint Consuls-General, Consuls, Vice-Consuls and other Consular agents, who shall reside in towns, ports and other places in each other's territory as may be agreed to. Consuls General, Consuls, Vice-Consuls and consular agents shall be provided with exequaturs or other valid authorization of their appointment. Such exequatur or authorization is liable tot be withdrawn by the country which issued it, if considered necessary. The reasons for the withdrawal shall be indicated wherever possible.

The person mentioned above shall enjoy on a reciprocal basis all the rights, privileges, exemptions and immunities that are accorded to persons of corresponding status of any other State.

Article V

The Government of Nepal shall be free to import, from or through the territory of India, arms, ammunition or warlike material and equipment necessary for to this arrangement shall be worked out by the two Governments acting in consultation.

Article VI

Each Government undertakes, in token of the neighbourly friendship between India and Nepal, to give to the nationals of the other, in its territory, national treatment with regard to participation in industrial and economic development of such territory and to the grant of concessions and contracts relating to such development.

Article VII

The Government of India and Nepal agree to grant, on reciprocal basis, to the nationals of one country in the territories of the other the same privileges in the matter residence, ownership of property, participation in trade and commerce, movement and privileges of a similar nature

Article VIII

So far as matters dealt with herein are concerned the Treaty cancels all previous treaties agreements, and engagements entered into on behalf of India between the British Government and the Government of. Nepal.

Article IX

This treaty shall come into force from the date of signature by both Governments.

Article X

The Treaty shall remain in force until it is terminated by either party by giving one year's notice.

Done in duplicate at Kathmandu this 31 day of July 1950

(Sd.) Chandreshwar Prasad Narain	(Sd.) Mohan Shamsher Jang Bahadur Rana
For the Government of India	For the Government of Nepal

Appendix IX

INDO-NEPAL TREATIES OF TRADE, OF TRANSIT, AND AGREEMENT FOR CO-OPERATION TO CONTROL UNAUTHORISED TRADE 1991

TREATY OF TRADE BETWEEN THE GOVERNMENT OF INDIA AND HIS MAJESTY'S GOVERNMENT OF NEPAL

The Government of India and His Majesty's Government of Nepal (hereinafter referred to as the Contracting Parties).

Being conscious of the need to fortify the traditional connection between the markets of the two countries.

Being animated by the desire to strengthen economic cooperation between them,

Impelled by the urge to develop their economies for their several and mutual benefit, and

Convinced of the benefits of mutual sharing of scientific and technical knowledge and experience to promote mutual trade,

Have resolved to conclude a Treaty of Trade in order to expand trade between their respective territories and encourage collaboration in economic development, and encourage collaboration in economic development, and

Have for this purpose appointed as their Plenipotentiaries the following persons, namely,

For the Government of India Shri P. Chidambaram, Minister of State for Commerce

For His Majesty's Govt. of Nepal Minister of Commerce

Who, having exchanged their full powers and found them good and in due form, have agreed as follows :

ARTICLE I

The Contracting Parties shall explore and undertake all measures, including technical cooperation, to promote, facilitate, expand and diversify trade between their two countries.

ARTICLE II

The Contracting Parties shall endeavour to grant maximum facilities and to undertake all necessary measures for the free and unhampered flow of goods, needed by one country from the other, to and from their respective territories.

ARTICLE III

Both the Contracting Parties shall accord unconditionally to each other treatment no less favourable than that accorded to any third country with respect to (a) customs duties and charges of any kind imposed on or in connection with importation and exportation, and (b) import regulations including quantitative restrictions.

ARTICLE IV

The Contracting Parties agree, on a reciprocal basis, to exempt from basic customs duty as well as from quantitative restrictions the import of such primary products as may be mutually agreed upon, from each other.

ARTICLE V

Notwithstanding the provisions of Article III and subject to such exceptions as may be made after consultation with His Majesty's Government of Nepal, the Government of India agree to promote the industrial development of Nepal through the grant on the basis of non-reciprocity of specially favourable treatment to imports into India of industrial products manufactured in Nepal in respect of customs duty and quantitative restrictions normally applicable to them.

ARTICLE VI

With a view to facilitating greater interchange of goods between the two countries, His Majesty's Government shall endeavour to exempt, wholly or partially, imports from India from customs duty and quantitative restrictions to the maximum extent compatible with their development needs and protection of their industries.

ARTICLE VII

Payment for transactions between the two countries will continue to be made in accordance with their respective foreign exchange laws, rules and regulations. The Contracting Parties agree to consult each other in the event of either of them experiencing difficulties in their mutual transactions with a view to resolving such difficulties.

ARTICLE VIII

The Contracting Parties agree to co-operate effectively with each other to prevent infringement and circumvention of the laws, rules and regulations of either country in regard to matters relating to foreign exchange and foreign trade.

ARTICLE IX

Notwithstanding the foregoing provisions, either Contracting Party may maintain or introduce such restrictions as are necessary for the purpose of:

1. protecting public morals,
2. protecting human, animal and plant life,
3. safeguarding national treasures,
4. safeguarding the implementation of laws relating to the import and export of gold and silver bullion, and
5. safeguarding such other interests as may be mutually agreed upon.

ARTICLE X

Nothing in this treaty shall prevent either Contracting Party from taking any measures which may be necessary for the protection of its essential security interests or in pursuance of general international conventions, whether already in existence or concluded hereafter, to which it is a party relating to transit, export or import of particular kinds of articles such as narcotics and psychotropic substances or in pursuance of general conventions intended to prevent infringement of industrial, literary or artistic property or relating to false marks, false indications of origin or other methods of unfair competition.

ARTICLE XI

In order to facilitate effective and harmonious implementation of this Treaty, the Contracting Parties shall consult each other regularly.

ARTICLE XII

This Treaty shall come into force on the 6 December, 1991, and shall remain in force for a period of five years. It may be renewed for further periods of five years, at a time, by mutual consent, subject to such modifications as may be agreed upon.

Done in duplicate in Hindi, Nepali and English languages, all the texts being equally authentic, at New Delhi on 6th December 1991. In case of doubt, the English text will prevail.

(P. CHIDAMBARAM)
Minister of State for Commerce For the Government of India

(GOPAL MAN SHRESTHA)
Minister of Commerce
For His Majesty's Govt. of Nepal

PROTOCOL TO THE TREATY OF TRADE

I. With Reference to Article I

1. It is understood that the trade between the two Contracting Parties shall be conducted through the mutually agreed routes as are mentioned in the Annexure A. Such mutually agreed routes would be subject to joint review as and when required.

2. It is further understood that the exports to and imports from each other of goods which are not subject to prohibitions or duties on exportation or importation shall continue to move through the traditional routes on the common border.

APPENDICES

II. With Reference to Article II

1. It is understood that all goods of Indian or Nepalese origin shall be allowed to move unhampered to Nepal or India respectively without being subjected to any quantitative restrictions, licensing or permit system with the following exceptions:

    1. (a) goods restricted for export to third countries,

    2. (b) goods subject to control on price for distribution or movement within the domestic market, and

    3. (c) goods prohibited for export to each other's territories to prevent deflection to third countries.

2. In order to facilitate the smooth flow of goods across the border, the list of commodities subject to restrictions/ prohibitions on exports to each other's territories shall be immediately communicated through diplomatic channels as and when such restrictions / prohibitions are imposed or relaxed.

3. It is further understood that when notifications regarding restrictions on exports to each other are issued, adequate provisions will be made therein to allow the export to each other of the goods which are already covered by Letter of Credit or goods which are already in transit and/ or booked through the railways or other public sector transport undertakings or goods which have already arrived at the border customs posts on the day of the notification.

4. In respect of goods falling under prohibited or restricted categories as mentioned in Para 1 above and where needed by one Contracting Party, the other shall authorise exports of such goods subject to specific annual quota allocations. Specific request list of such goods shall be furnished to each other by the end of November, and specific quota allocations for the following calendar year shall be made by the end of December with due regard to the supply availability and the overall need of the other Contracting Party. The quota list may be jointly reviewed as and when necessary.

5. The Contracting Parties shall take appropriate measures and co-operate with each other to prevent unauthorised import in excess

of the quota of goods the export of which is prohibited or restricted from the territory of the other Contracting Party.

III With reference to Article III

1. The Government of India will allow to His Majesty's Government of Nepal payment of the excise and other duties collected by the Government of India on goods produced in India and exported to Nepal provided that:

   (i) such payment shall not exceed the import duties and like charges levied by His Majesty's Government of Nepal on similar goods imported from any other country, and

   (ii) His Majesty's Government of Nepal shall not collect from the importer of the said Indian goods so much of the import duty and like charges as is equal to the payment allowed by the Government of India.

IV. With Reference to Article IV

1. The following primary products would be eligible for preferential treatment :

   1. Agriculture, horticulture and forest produce and minerals which have not undergone any processing,

   2. Rice, pulses and flour,

   3. Timber,

   4. Jaggery (gur and shakar)

   5. Animals, birds and fish,

   6. Bees, bees-wax and honey,

   7. Raw wool, goat hair, and bones as are used in the manufacture of bone-meal,

   8. Milk, home made products of milk and eggs,

   9. Ghani-produced oil and oilcakes,

Appendices

10. Ayurvedic and herbal medicines,

11. Articles produced by village artisans as are mainly used in villages,

12. Akara,

13. Yak Tail,

14. Any other primary products which may be mutually agreed upon.

2. It is understood that in the matter of internal taxes or charges the movement of primary products of either Contracting Party to any market destinations in the territory of the other shall be accorded treatment no less favourable than that accorded to the movement of its own primary products within its territory.

3. It is also understood that the aforesaid provisions will not preclude a Contracting Party from taking any measures which it may deem necessary on the exportation of primary products to the other.

V. With Reference to Article V

1. (i) The Government of India will provide access to the Indian market free of basic and auxiliary customs duty and quantitative restrictions. Generally, for all manufactured articles which contain not less than eight per cent of Nepalese materials of Nepalese and Indian materials.

(ii) Further, the Government of India will provide access to the Indian market, on case to case basis, free of basic and auxiliary customs duty and quantitative restrictions for manufactured articles which contain not less than fifty five per cent of Nepalese materials or Nepalese and Indian materials.

2. Further, when such articles are manufactured in "small" units in Nepal, the "additional" duty on these articles will be equivalent to the rates of excise duty applicable under the Indian Customs and Central Excise Tariff to articles produced in similar units in India.

3. In regard to "additional" duty collected by the Government of

India in respect of manufactured in "small" units : Wherever it is established that the cost of production of an article is higher in Nepal than the cost of production in a corresponding unit in India, a sum representing such difference in the cost of production, but not exceeding 25 per cent of the "additional" duty collected by the Government of India, will be paid to his Majesty's Government of Nepal provided :

(a) Such manufactured articles contain not less than eighty percent of Nepalese and Indian materials, and

(b) His Majesty's Government of Nepal have given assistance to the same extent to the (manufacturer, exporter).

4. Procedures to determine the eligibility of industrial products to these concessions and for the verification of the values of different components of Nepalese industrial products shall be as already in force under the 1978 Indo-Nepal Treaty of Trade Changes, if any, in the procedures which may be considered necessary may be agreed upon mutually.

5. List of articles produced in Nepal already exempted from "basic and auxiliary" customs duty and quantitative restrictions under provisions of para 1 above is at Annexure "B".

6. In the case of other manufactured articles in which the value of Nepalese and Indian materials including labour added in Nepal is at least 40 percent of the ex-factory price, the Government of India will allow the articles on case by case basis for following preferential treatment keeping in mind the need for expeditious clearance in the Indian market :

(a) barring exceptional circumstances, exemption from quantitative restriction, and/or

(b) tariff concessions to the extent of fifty percent of the MFN rate of import duty where the value added in such articles is less than eighty percent but more than forty percent of the ex-factory price.

7. His Majesty's Government will furnish the request list of the

articles eligible for preferential access to the Indian market as per the Para 6 above as and when required and on receipt of which the Government of India will communicate expeditiously to His Majesty's Government the scope of preferential treatment offered to such articles.

8. It is also understood that in the case of other manufactured articles in which the value of Nepalese and Indian materials and labour added in Nepal is less than forty percent of the ex-factory price, the Government of India will provide normal access to the Indian market consistent with its import regime and MFN treatment accorded.

9. Where for social and economic reasons, the import of an item into India is permitted only through public sector agencies or where the import of an item is prohibited under the Indian Trade Control regulations, the Government of India will consider any request of His Majesty's Government of Nepal for relaxation and may permit the import of such an item from Nepal in such manner as may be found to be suitable.

10. For the purpose of calculation of import duties customs valuation procedures, as prescribed under the Indian Customs Act, will be followed.

11. Export of articles eligible for preferential treatment in accordance with above mentioned paragraph shall be covered by a certificate from His Majesty's Government of Nepal or an authority designated by it which shall certify the extent of material component or value added involved as the case may be.

VI. With Reference to Article VI

His Majesty's Government of Nepal, with a view to continuing preferences given to Indian exports, will waive additional customs duty on all Indian exports during the validity of the Treaty.

IX. New Protocol to Article IX of the Treaty has been introduced with effect from 6.3.2002 (Attached).

AGREED ROUTES FOR MUTUAL TRADE
ANNEXURE "A"

1. Pashupatinagar/Sukhia Pokhari
2. Kakarbhitta/naxalbari
3. Bhadrapur/Galgalia
4. Biratnagar/Jogbani
5. Setobandha/Bhimnagar
6. Rajbiraj/Kunauli
   Siraha, Janakpur/Jayanagar
7. Jaleswar/Bhitamore (Sursand)
8. Malangawa/Sonabarsa
9. Gaur/Bairgania
10. Birgunj/Raxaul
11. Bhairahawa/Nautanwa
12. Taulihawa/Khunwa
13. Krishnanagar/Barhni
14. Koilabas/Jarwa
15. Nepalgunj/Nepalgunj
16. Road Rajapur/Katerniyaghat
17. Prithvipur/Sati (Kailali)/Tikonia
18. Dhangadhi/Gauriphanta
19. Mahendranagar/Banbasa
20. Mahakali/Jhulaghat (Pithoraghar)
21. Darchula/Dharchula

APPENDICES

ANNEXURE "B"

LIST OF NEPALESE INDUSTRIAL PRODUCTS WHICH HAVE BEEN ALLOWED PREFERENTIAL ENTRY INTO INDIA UNDER NOTIFICATION NO.203/90- CUSTOMS (AS ON 6th DECEMBER, 1991)

Sr. No. Description of Goods

1. Biscuits
2. Refined Ghee
3. High Boiled Sweets
4. Salseed Oil, Rice Bran Oil, Salseed Extraction and Rice Extraction
5. Straw Board
6. Plywood
7. Magnesite
8. Marble Blocks, Slabs and Chips
9. Wet Blue Chrome Tanned Goat Skins
10. Cast Iron Goods
11. Raw Talc
12. Ice Blocks
13. Wooden Articles and furniture
14. Katha and Kutch
15. Wheat Bran
16. Jute Manufactures-all sorts
17. Mustard Oil
18. Resin

19. Oil Cakes
20. Chuni, Bhusi & Akra
21. Hnadicrafts and Handlooms
22. Linseed Oil
23. Match Splints
24. Ground Talc (other than cosmetic grade)
25. Saw Dust
26. Rice Bran
27. Sugar
28. Slate
29. Powdered Lime
30. Cattle and Poultry Feed
31. Split crust (Cow and Buff)
32. Wet Blue Hides (Cow and Buff)
33. Wet Blue Split (Cow and Buff)
34. Vegetable Tanned Buff Sole Leather
35. Chrome Upper and & Lining Leather
36. Leather Board
37. Ginger Oil
38. Fruit Jam, Jelly and Squash
39. Lemon Barley
40. Vinegar
41. Pineapple Crush
42. rose Syrup and Khus Syrup

Appendices

43. Tomato Sauce and Tomato Ketchup

44. Golden Mist Marmalade

45. Noddles and Spaggheti

46. Hides and Skins (processed and semi processed)

47. Redried Tobacco (Non-processed)

48. Footwear and Closed Leather Uppers

49. Mama Snacks (Corn puff)

50. Pan Masala that is to say, any preparation containing betal nuts and any one or more of other ingredients such as lime, katha (catechu), cardamom, copra, menthol and tobacco.

51. Emery Cloth

52. Emery Paper

53. Sand Paper

54. Rosin

55. Turpentine

56. Dressed Bristles

57. Paint Brushes

58. Wood Veneer

59. Pasteurised Butter

60. Chocolate pastry

61. Coconut Cakes

62. Dead Burnt Magnesite

63. Linchin Resinoid

64. Pineapple Pulp

65. Orange juice
66. Orange Extracts
67. Lead Pencils
68. Writing and Printing Papers
69. Solid Wood Panel Door
70. Solid Wood Parquet
71. Fruit Juices packed in bottles or cans, made of soft steel Plate with a coating of pure tin.
72. Tomato juice packed in bottles or cans made of soft steel plate with a coating of pure tin.
73. Pine apple slices packed in cans made of soft steel plates with a coating of pure tin.
74. Tomato Puree packed in cans made of soft steel plate with a coating of pure tin.
75. Wire Nails
76. Barbed Wire
77. Aluminium Utensils
78. Laundry Soap
79. Cube Sugar
80. Terry-Towel and Terry-Towel Cloth
81. Winter Green Oil
82. Abies Oil
83. Artemisia Oil
84. Juniper Oil
85. Balladone Extracts

86. Palmarosa Oil

87. Zanthoxyluim Oil

88. Bidi

89. Chewing Gum

90. Bubble Gum

91. Asbestos Cement Pipes

These products have been exempted from submission of proformae.

TREATY OF TRANSIT BETWEEN THE GOVERNMENT OF INDIA AND HIS MAJESTY'S GOVERNMENT OF NEPAL

The Government of India and His Majesty's Government of Nepal (hereinafter also referred to as the Contracting Parties).

Animated by the desired to maintain, develop and strengthen the existing friendly relations and cooperation between the two countries,

Recognising that Nepal as a land-locked country needs access to and from the sea to promote its international trade,

And recognizing the need to facilitate the traffic in transit through their territories,

Having resolved to conclude a Treaty of Transit, and

Have for this purpose appointed as their plenipotentiaries the following persons namely.

Shri P. Chidambaram
Minister of State for Commerce For Government of India

Shri Gopal Man Shrestha Minister of Commerce for His Majesty's Government of Nepal

Who, having exchanged their full powers, and found them good and in due form, have agreed as follows :

ARTICLE I

The Contracting Parties shall accord to "traffic in transit" freedom of transit across their respective territories through routes mutually agreed upon. No distinction shall be made which is based on flag of vessels, the places of origin, departure, entry, exit, destination, ownership of goods or vessels.

ARTICLE II

(a) Each Contracting Parties shall accord to "traffic in transit" freedom of transit across their respective territories through routes mutually agreed upon. No distinction shall be made which is based on flag of vessels, the places of origin, departure, entry, exit, destination, ownership of goods or vessels.

(b) Nothing in this Treaty shall prevent either Contracting Party from taking any measures which may be necessary for the protection of its essential security interests.

ARTICLE III

The term "traffic in transit" means the passage of goods including unaccompanied baggage across the territory of a Contracting Party when the passage is a portion of a complete journey which begins or terminates within the territory of the other Contracting Party. The transshipment, warehousing, breaking bulk and change in the mode of transport of such goods as well as the assembly, dis-assembly or re-assembly of machinery and bulky goods outside the definition of "traffic in transit" provided any such operation is undertaken solely for the convenience of transportation. Nothing in this Article shall be construed as imposing an obligation on either Contracting Party to establish or permit the establishment of permanent facilities on its territory for such assembly, dis- assembly or re-assembly.

ARTICLE IV

Traffic in transit shall be exempt from customs duties and from all transit duties or other charges except reasonable charges for transportation and such other charges as are commensus with the costs of services rendered in respect of such transit.

ARTICLE V

For convenience of traffic in transit the Contracting Parties agree to provide at point or points of entry or exit, on such terms as may be mutually agreed upon and subject to their relevant laws and regulations prevailing in either country, warehouses or sheds, for the storage of traffic in transit awaiting customs clearance before onward transmission.

ARTICLE VI

Traffic in transit shall be subject to the procedure laid down in the Protocol hereto annexed and as modified by mutual agreement. Except in cases of failure to comply with the procedure prescribed, such traffic in transit shall not be subject to avoidable delays or restrictions.

ARTICLE VII

In order to enjoy the freedom of the high seas, merchant ships sailing under the flag of Nepal shall be accorded, subject to Indian laws and regulations, treatment no less favourable than that accorded to ships of any other foreign country in respect of matters relating to navigation, entry in to and departure from the ports, use of ports and harbour facilities, as well as loading and unloading dues, taxes and other levies, except that the provisions of this Article shall not extend to coastal trade.

ARTICLE VIII

Notwithstanding the foregoing provisions, either Contracting Party may maintain or introduce such measures or restrictions as are necessary for the purpose of :

1. (i) Protecting public morals;
2. (ii) Protecting human, animal and plant life;
3. (iii) Safeguarding the implementation of laws relating to the import and export of gold and other silver bullion; and
4. (iv) Safeguarding such other interests as may be mutually agreed upon.

ARTICLE IX

Nothing in this Treaty shall prevent either Contracting party from taking any measures which may be necessary in pursuance of general international conventions, whether already in existence or concluded hereafter, to which it is a party relating to transit, export or import of particular kinds of article such as narcotics and psychotropic substances or in pursuance of general conventions intended to prevent infringement of industrial, literary or artistic property or relating to false marks, false indications of foreign or other methods of unfair competition.

ARTICLE X

In order to facilitate effective and harmonious implementation of this Treaty the Contracting Parties shall consult each other regularly.

ARTICLE XI

This Treaty shall enter into force on the 6 December 1991 and shall remain in force for a period of seven years. It may be renewed for further periods of seven years by mutual consent, subject to such modifications as may be agreed upon.

Done in duplicate in Hindi, Nepali and English languages, all the texts being equally authentic, at New Delhi on the 6th December 1991. In case of doubt, the English text will prevail.

(P. Chidambaram),	(Gopal Man Shrestha),
Minister of State for Commerce	Minister of Commerce
For Government of India	for His Majesty's Government of Nepal

APPENDICES

PROTOCOL TO THE TREATY OF TRANSIT BETWEEN INDIA AND NEPAL

With Reference to Article V

1. The following warehouses, sheds and open space, or such other warehouses, sheds and open space as the Trustees of the Port of Calcutta may offer in lieu thereof, shall be made available for the storage of transit cargo (other than hazardous goods) meant for transit to and from Nepal through India in accordance with the procedure contained in the Memorandum to the Protocol :

(i) COVERED ACCOMMODATION

'A" Shed Kidderpore Docks — Covering approximately 3135 sq. metres (including 'A' Annex)

Shed No. 25, Kidderpore — Covering approximately 4425 sq. metres.

Calcutta Jetty Shed No. 8 — Ground Floor

(ii) OPEN SPACE

Open land at Circular Garden Reach Road – Covering approximately 4332 sq. metres.

Residential cum office land — Covering approximately 2000.00 sq. metres. Space at Haldia.

Open land space at Haldia - Covering approximately 6985.00 sq. metres Dock interior zone.

2. The above storage facilities shall be given on lease by the Trustees of the Port of Calcutta (hereinafter referred to as the Trustees) to an undertaking incorporated in accordance with the relevant Indian laws and designated by His Majesty's Government of Nepal for this purpose (hereinafter referred to as the Lessee).

3. The terms of the leases to be entered into between the Trustees and 'Lessee' shall conform to the 'Long-term Lease-Godown' and 'Commercial Lease-land long-term' of the Trustees. The leases will be 'for twenty-five years.

4. Kidderpore Docks berth No. 25 shall be assigned by Calcutta Port Trust as a preferential berth to the lessee on commercial terms as applicable from time to time to Shipping Lines of India, if such a lease is finalised within six months of the signing of the treaty. If, however, this option is not exercised within this period, charter vessels carrying traffic in transit of Nepal may be assigned to 25 K.P.D berth on a priority basis, to the extent possible.

5. The lease rent shall be determined in accordance with the Schedules of Rent Charges as determined by the Trustees-in-meeting from time to time.

6. The transit cargo shall be subject to the levy of all charges by the Trustees in accordance with their Schedule of Charges in force from time to time.

7. The Lessee would be permitted to own/or operate a number of trucks and barges in the Port Area in connection with the storage of cargo in transit in the said areas, subject to compliance with the normal rules and regulations applicable to trucks and barges plying in the Port Area.

8. The Collector of Customs, Calcutta, in accordance with the relevant provisions of the laws and regulations, will provide the lessee for a customs house agent's licence for the clearance at the Port of Calcutta of traffic in transit from and to Nepal. If a licence is also required from the Port of Calcutta for this work, Calcutta Port Trust will provide such licence in accordance with the relevant provisions of their bye-laws/regulations.

9. The owner of gods or the lessee, if authorized by owner, may under the supervision of the proper officer of the Indian Customs :

1. (i) Inspect the gods,

2. (ii) Separate damaged or deteriorated goods from the rest.

3. (iii) Sort the goods or change their containers for the purpose of preservation for onward transmission.

4. (iv) Deal with the goods and their containers in such a manner as may be necessary to prevent loss or deterioration or damage to the goods.

Appendices

10. The warehouses shall function during the normal working hours under the supervision of officers to be provided by the Calcutta Custom House. Where, however, such functioning is necessary outside the office hours, officers for supervision would be provided by the said Customs House on payment of the prescribed fees.

With Reference to Article VI

1. All traffic in transit shall –
   (i) pass only through the following routes :

   (a) Calcutta Galgalia

   (b) Calcutta Jogbani

   (c) Calcutta Bhimnagar

   (d) Calcutta Jayanagar

   (e) Calcutta Raxual

   (f) Calcutta Nautanwa

   (g) Calcutta Barhni

   (h) Calcutta Nepalgunj Road

   (i) Calcutta Gauri-Phanta

   (j) Calcutta Banbasa

   (k) Calcutta Tikonia

   (l) Calcutta Jarwa

   (m) Calcutta Bhitamore (Sitamarhi)

   (n) Calcutta Naxalbari (Panitanki)

   (o) Calcutta Sukhiya Pokhari

Provided that:

    (a) These routes may be discontinued or new ones added by mutual agreement.

    (b) (i) Bulk traffic such as fertilizers, cement, etc. moving by rail shall pass through Calcutta Narayanpur Anant route or any other agreed route subject to prior intimation being given to Customs as and when such movements are anticipated.

    (ii) Comply with the procedure as set out in the memorandum annexed hereto,

    (iii) Comply with any other detailed regulations which may be prescribed through mutual consultation by the Contracting Parties in keeping with the nature of the commodity and the need for expeditious movement and the safety of transport.

2. Whenever en route it becomes necessary to break bulk in respect of consignments in transit, such breaking shall be done only under the supervision of the appropriate officials of the Indian Customs.

3. All goods intended for removal in transit to Nepal while in the process of removal to or from the warehouses or other storage places that may be leased out in Calcutta Port for the storage of such goods and also while in storage or under the process of packing, sorting and separation etc. in such warehouses or places, shall be subject to relevant Indian laws and regulations.

4. The procedure in the foregoing paragraphs shall apply mutates mutandis to road transport with the following modifications:

    a) Arms, ammunition and hazardous cargo shall not be allowed to be transported by road.

NOTE : With reference to hazardous cargo, exception could be permitted as may be mutually agreed.

    b) The truck shall have a pilfer-proof container conforming to specifications to be mutually agreed upon which is capable of being locked and sealed. The Containers shall be locked by the locks of Indian Customs.

APPENDICES

c) The individual packages shall be sealed by Indian Customs.

d) Conditions at (b) and (c) above shall not apply to non-sensitive bulk items as may be mutually agreed upon.

e) Sealing of individual packages may be dispensed with when they are imported packed in recognized containers, provided the entire contents of the container are consigned to the same consignee and container is sealed and the provision of (b) above is complied with.

f) If the truck breaks down, the nearest Customs Officer shall be approached with least possible delay.

g) Any other mutually agreed modifications that may be considered necessary from time to time in respect of the procedure for road transport operation.

5. Respecting each other's relevant laws, it is agreed that the Contracting Parties will take all steps to prevent detection of their mutual trade to third countries and to ensure compliance with the procedure for the transit of goods across their territories.

6. In order to facilitate the movement of traffic in transit, additional means of transport and facilities, mutually agreed upon, may be added.

MEMORANDUM

In pursuance of and subject to the provisions of the Protocol to the Treaty of Transit, His Majesty's Government of Nepal and the Government of India agree that the following detailed procedure shall apply to traffic in transit:

IMPORT PROCEDURE

When goods are imported from third countries for Nepal in transit through India, the following procedure shall be observed at the Indian port of entry (hereinafter called the Customs House):

1.(a) Transit of consumer goods and specialised materials for consumer goods imported for Nepal shall be allowed against import licences issued by HMG.

(b) In case of goods other than those referred to in (a) above, the royal

Nepalese Consul General at Calcutta shall furnish the following certificate on the Customs Transit Declaration :

"I have verified that the gods specified in this Declaration and of the quantity and value specified herein have been permitted to be imported by His Majesty's Government of Nepal under Licence No. .... dated....................

NOTE : I *His Majesty's Government will arrange to supply through the Indian Embassy at Kathmandu to the Collectors of Customs concerned, the specimen signature of official/officials who sign His Majesty's Government's import licences. It will also arrange to have one copy each of import licences issued by it for such goods, sent direct to the Collector of Customs concerned :*

NOTE : II *This requirement will not apply in case of goods for the import of which into Nepal no licence is required under the laws of HMG of Nepal.*

2. At the Customs House, the importer or his agent (hereinafter referred to as the importer) shall present a Customs Transit Declaration containing the following :

    a) Ship's name, Rotation No. and Line No.,

    b) Name and address of the importer,

    c) No., Description, Marks and Serial Nos. of the packages,

    d) Country of consignment, origin, if different,

    e) Description of goods,

    f) Quantity of goods,

    g) Value of goods,

    h) HMG' s import licence No. and date,

    i) Route of transit,

    j) A declaration at the end in the following words :

"I/We declared that all the goods entered herein are for Nepal in transit through India and shall not be diverted enroute to India or retained in India.

Appendices

"I/We declared that all the entries made therein above are true and correct to the best of my/our knowledge and belief."

Signature

3. The Customs Transit Declaration shall be made in sextuplicate. All copies along with Nepal Import Licence wherever required, shall be presented to the Customs House. The copy of the Nepal Import Licence so presented shall be compared by the Customs House with the copy received directly from HMG of Nepal.

4. Consumer goods and specialised materials for consumer goods must be removed to Nepal sheds within free time, if not already put in wagons. An authorization with removal instructions of the owner for the purpose shall be necessary for removal. The Government of India will continue the arrangement with the Trustees of the Port of Calcutta for increasing the free time for Nepal's transit cargo including containerized cargo to 7 days.

5. The Customs House shall make a percentage examination of the goods to check whether the goods are in accordance with the Customs Transit Declaration and conform to the import licence wherever such licence is required. Goods for Nepal as covered by the said licence and also in accordance with the Customs Transit Declaration shall be approved for onward transmission. However, in making such examination, avoidable delays shall be curtailed to the utmost in order to expedite the traffic-in-transit.

NOTE : The percentage examination referred to here means that a percentage of the total packages in a consignment will be selected for examination and not that a percentage of the contents of everyone of the package comprised in the consignment will be examined.

6. The good shall be transported from the Customs Port of entry to the border post in closed railway wagons or in pilfer-proof containers (to be provided by the importer) which can be securely locked. The containers or wagons, as the case may be, shall be locked and dully sealed after the above examination. Individual packages in such wagons or containers shall not be sealed except where consumer goods or specialised materials for consumer goods are being transported or where the goods are to go to Nepal by a route where the railway line does not reach upto the last town of the border.

7. Where goods cannot be transported in closed wagons, and have to be transported in open wagons or flats, detailed identifying particulars shall be recorded in the Customs Transit Declaration.

8. "Small" consignments of traffic in transit will be accepted for booking by railway from one of the agreed warehouses leased to Nepal Transit and Warehousing Company Ltd. provided the minimum load condition as applicable in Indian Railways is satisfied.

9. The goods shall be covered by an insurance policy and/or such legally binding undertaking to the satisfaction of the Collector of Customs, Calcutta, in the manner indicated below :

(a) Goods moving by rail up to the border shall be covered by an insurance policy for an amount equal to the Indian Customs Duty on such goods. This policy shall be assigned to the Collector of Customs, Calcutta, and the amount shall become payable to the Collector in the event of the goods not reaching Nepal.

(b) Goods moving by road in trucks belonging to Nepal Transit & Warehousing Company Ltd., or Nepal Transport Corporation shall be covered by an insurance policy for an amount equal to the Indian Customs duty on such goods. This policy shall be assigned to the Collector of Customs, Calcutta, and the amount shall become payable to the Collector in the event of the goods, not reaching Nepal. In addition, Nepal Transit and Warehousing Company Ltd., shall give an undertaking to the Collector of Customs, Calcutta to pay the difference between the Company Ltd., shall give an undertaking to the Collector of Customs, Calcutta, to pay the difference between the market value of goods in India and their c.i.f. value plus Indian Customs duty in the event of the goods not reaching Nepal.

(c) Goods moving by road in trucks other than those mentioned at (b) above shall be insured for an amount equal to the difference between the market value of the goods in India and their c.i.f. value. This policy shall be assigned to the Collector of Customs, Calcutta, and the amount shall become payable to the Collector in the event of the goods not reaching Nepal.

Appendices

NOTES : 1. In respect of goods belonging and consigned to His Majesty's Government of Nepal under (a) and (b) above no insurance shall be required provided an undertaking or a further undertaking, as the case may be, is given by Nepal Transit and Warehousing Company Ltd., in lieu of such insurance.

2. No such requirement will be necessary in respect of goods carried by air without transshipment enroute or in such cases as may be mutually agreed upon.

3. In the event of goods carried by rail not reaching the booked destination, Indian Railways shall, where liable as carriers under the Indian Railways Act, pay the c.i.f price to the importer.

10. After the Customs House is satisfied as regards the checks contemplated in the preceding paragraphs, it shall endorse all the copies of the Customs Transit Declaration. The original copy shall be handed over to the importer. The duplicate and triplicate will be sent by post to the Indian Border Customs Officer and the remaining copies shall be retained by the Customs House. In order to avoid delay in postal transmission, duplicate and triplicate copies of the C.T.D. along with copy of the original railway receipt shall be handed over to the importer or his authorized representative in a sealed cover, if he so desires. This facility shall however be denied to the importer who defaults in the production of these documents within a reasonable time to the Indian Border Customs Officer.

11. In case of any suspicion of pilferages, traffic-in-transit shall be subject to checks by the Indian Customs during the period that they are in transit, as many be necessary, particularly at the point of railway transshipment from broad-gauge to metre-gauge.

12. On arrival of goods in transit at the border railway station, the sealed wagons or the sealed containers, as the case may be, shall be presented to the Indian Customs Officer at the station, shall be presented to the Indian Customs Officer at the station, who shall examine the seals and locks and, if satisfied, shall permit the unloading or breaking of bulk, as the case may be, under his supervision. The importer shall present the original copy of the Customs Transit Declaration duly endorsed by the Indian Custom House of entry, to the Indian Customs Border Officer, who shall compare the original copy with the duplicate and triplicate received by him and

will, in cases where the seals and the locks on the wagons or containers and on the packages where required under para 6 are intact, identify the packages with the corresponding Customs Declaration, In cases where the seals and locks on the wagons or on the containers or on the packages are not intact, or there is suspicion otherwise, he may examine the contents. The goods shall be delivered by the railway only after clearance as above by the Indian Customs Officer at the border station. The Indian Customs Officer shall thereafter through such escorts. The Indian Customs Officer shall thereafter through such escorts or supervision as may be necessary ensure that the goods cross the border and reach Nepal. He, or in cases where there is an Indian Officer posted right at the border, such officer will certify on the copies of the Customs Transit Declaration that the goods have crossed in the Nepal. The Indian Customs Officers shall then hand over the original copy of the Customs Transit Declaration to the importer, send the duplicate to the Indian Custom House at the port of entry, send the triplicate to the Nepalese Customs Officer at the corresponding Nepalese post and after it is received back duly endorsed by the Nepalese Customs Officer, retain it for his records.

13. If a consignment in transit is received at destination in more than one lot, the separate losts of the consignment covered by one Customs Transit Declaration may be presented in separate lots and the Indian Customs Officer at the border shall release the goods so presented after necessary examination and check of relevant documents and goods and after making the necessary endorsement. In such a case, the Indian Customs Officer, at the border shall send the triplicate copy of Customs Transit Declaration to the Nepalese Customs Officer at the corresponding Nepalese post only after release of the entire consignment as covered by the Customs Transit Declaration.

14. In cases where the duplicate and triplicate copies of the Customs Transit Declaration are not received at the Customs Office of exit, the Indian Customs Office will, by telephonic or other quick means of communication with the Customs Office of entry seek confirmation to ensure against delay and them on the basis of aforesaid confirmation allow dispatch of goods.

15. The Nepalese Customs Officer shall:

(i) endorse a certificate over his signature and authenticate it under customs stamp on the original copy of the Nepal import licence, if any,

Appendices

and the Customs Transit declaration that the packages correspond in all respects with the particulars shown in the declaration and in all material respects with the Nepal import licence and that the goods have been cleared from Nepalese Customs custody for entry into Nepal;

(ii) return the original copy of the Declaration and the original copy of the Nepal import licence, if any, to the importer or his agent;

(iii) return the triplicate copy duly endorsed to the authorized official of Land Customs and Central Excise after the goods have crossed the Nepalese border customs post.

16. The importer will present to the Assistant Collector of Customs the original Customs Transit Declaration duly certified by the authorized officer of Land Customs and Excise and the Nepalese Customs Officer to the effect that the goods have crossed into Nepal. The original Declaration should reach the Assistant Collector of Customs concerned within one month of the date on which transit was allowed at the Indian Port importation, or such extended time as the Assistant Collector of Customs might allow. For every week or part thereof delay in presenting the original Customs Transit Declaration duly certified as above, the importer shall pay a sum of Re. 1/- for every Rs. 1000/- of the Indian market price of the goods.

EXPORT PROCEDURE

When gods from Nepal are cleared from Nepalese Customs custody for export to third countries in transit through India, the exporter or his agent (hereinafter referred to as the exporter) shall be required to observe the following procedure at the corresponding Indian Border Customs Post:

1. The Senior – most officer incharge of the Nepalese Customs Office at the border shall furnish the following certificate on the Customs Transit Declaration:

'I have verified that the gods specified in this Declaration and of the quantity and value specified herein have been permitted to be exported by His Majesty's Government of Nepal under licence No. .... dated...............'

2. The exporter shall prepare the Customs Transit Declaration in

quadruplicate and shall present it to the Indian Customs Officer at the Customs Port through which the goods are to enter India. The Customs Transit Declaration shall contain the following particulars :

(a) Name and address of the Exporter

(b) No., description, marks and serial nos. of the packages.

(c) Country to which consigned

(d) Description of Goods

(e) Quantity of goods

(f) Value of goods

(g) HMG's Export Licence No. and date

(h) Country of origin of the goods

(i) Indian Customs Office of entry from Nepal

(j) A declaration at the end in the following words:

"I/We declare that the goods entered herein are not of Indian origin, are for export from Nepal to countries other than India and shall not be diverted enroute to India or retained in India".

"I/We declared that all the entries made above true and correct to the best of my/our knowledge and belief".

Signature

3. The Indian Customs Officer at the point of entry into India shall make such examination of packages and the contents as may be necessary to check whether:

    (i) the goods are in accordance with the Customs Transit Declaration :

    (ii) the goods are such as have been specified by the Government of India as being liable to pilferage enroute having regard to the duty and restrictions, if any, to which they are liable on import into India;

Appendices

(iii) they are of origin as declared in the Customs Declaration Form.

4. After the necessary checks, the Indian Customs Officer at the border shall endorse all the CTDs. They shall hand over original to the exporter and send the duplicate and triplicate by post to the Collector of Customs, Calcutta. In order to avoid delay in postal transmission, duplicate and triplicate copies of CTDs shall be handed over to the exporter or his authorized representative in a sealed cover, if he so desired. This facility shall, however, be denied to the exporter who defaults in the production of these documents within reasonable period to the Indian Customs House at the port of exit. The quadruplicate shall be retained by the Indian Customs Officer at the border.

5. The goods specified in sub-paragraph (ii) of paragraph 3 above shall be transported from the Indian Customs border post to Calcutta port in closed railway wagons or in pilfer- proof containers (to be provided by the exporter) which can be securely locked. The containers or wagons, as the case may be, shall be locked and duly sealed after the examination by the border Customs Officer.

6. Where the goods cannot be sent in closed wagons and have to be transported in open wagons or flats, detailed description, particulars and specifications thereof shall be recorded in the Customs Transit Declaration.

7. After the verification as contemplated in preceding paragraphs has been completed by the Indian Customs official at the border, he shall endorse all the copies of the declaration and where sealing has been done, given necessary indication thereof on the relevant Customs Transit Declaration and allow the movement of goods to Calcutta Port. He shall hand over the original copy of the Declaration to the exporter and send the duplicate and triplicate by post to the Collector of Customs, Calcutta and retain the quadruplicate copy with him.

8. The goods specified in sub para (ii) of para 3 above shall be covered by an insurance policy and/or such legally binding undertaking to the satisfaction of the concerned Collector of Customs in the manner indicate below:

(a) Goods moving by rail from the border shall be covered by an insurance policy for an amount equal to the Indian Customs duty on such goods. This policy shall be assigned to the concerned

Collector of Customs and the amount shall become payable to the Collector in the event of the goods not reaching Calcutta Customs.

(b) Goods moving by road in trucks belonging to Nepal Transit and Warehousing Co. Ltd or Nepal Transport Corporation shall be covered by an insurance policy for an amount equal to the Indian Customs duty on such goods. This policy shall be assigned to the concerned Collector of Customs, and the amount shall become payable to the Collector in the event of the goods not reaching Calcutta Customs. In addition, Nepal Transit and Warehousing Co Ltd. shall give an undertaking to the concerned Collector of Customs to pay the difference between the market value of goods in India and their c.i.f. value plus Indian Customs duty in the event of the goods not reaching Calcutta Customs.

(c) Goods moving by road in trucks other than those mentioned at (b) above shall be insured for an amount equal to the difference between the market value of the goods in India and their c.i.f. value. This policy shall be assigned t the concerned Collector of Customs and the amount shall become payable to the Collector in the event of the goods not reaching Calcutta Customs.

Note: 1. In respect of goods belonging to and consigned by His Majesty's Government of Nepal under (a) and (b) above no insurance shall be required provided an undertaking or a further undertaking, as the case may be, is given by Nepal Transit and Warehousing Co. Ltd. in lieu of such insurance.

2. No such requirement will be necessary in respect of goods carried by air without transshipment enroute or in such cases as may be mutually agreed upon.

3. In the event of goods carried by rail not reaching the booked destination, Indian Railways shall, where liable as carriers under the Indian Railways Act pay the c.i.f price to the exporter.

9. In the case of any suspicion of pilferage, the goods specified in sub-para (ii) of para 3 above shall, while in transit through India, be subject to such checks by the Indian Customs as may be necessary particularly at the point of railway transshipment from metre-gauge to broad-gauge.

APPENDICES

10. On arrival of goods at Calcutta Port, the exporter shall present the original copy of the Customs Transit Declaration duly endorsed by the Customs Border Office to the Customs House. This copy shall be compared by the Customs House with the duplicate and triplicate received by it from the border. In case of goods which have moved under seals and locks, the Customs House shall check the seals and locks and where there is suspicion that they have been tampered with will examine the goods to identify them with the corresponding Customs Transit Declaration. After the verification as contemplated in this paragraph is completed by the Customs Houses, it shall permit the export of the goods and will in case of goods specified in sub-para (ii) of para 3 ensure that these are duly shipped. After the goods have been shipped, the Customs House shall endorse all the copies of the Customs Transit Declaration, hand over the original to the exporter and send the triplicate copy to the Indian Customs Border and Office and retain the duplicate.

11. Where export cargo is shut out, it will be removed to the warehouse leased out to Nepal Transit and Warehousing Co. Ltd., on filing of such removal instructions by the exporter or his authorized agents.

AGREEMENT OF COOPERATION BETWEEN GOVERNMENT OF INDIA AND HIS MAJESTY'S GOVERNMENT OF NEPAL TO CONTROL UNAUTHORISED TRADE

The Government of India and His Majesty's Government of Nepal (hereinafter also referred to as the Contracting Parties).

KEEN to sustain the good neighbourlines through mutually beneficial measures at their common border which is free fro movement of persons and goods. Have agreed as follows :

Article I

The Contracting Parties, while recognizing that there is a long and open border between the two countries and there is free movement of persons and goods across the border and noting that they have the right to pursue independent foreign trade policies, agree that either of them would take all such measures as are necessary to ensure that the economic interests of the other party are not adversely affected through unauthorised trade between the two countries.

Article II

The Contracting Parties agree to cooperate effectively with each other, to prevent infringement and circumvention of the laws, rules and regulations of either country in regard to matters relating to Customs, Narcotics and Psychotropic Substances, Foreign Exchange and Foreign Trade and shall for this purpose assist each other in such matters as consultation, enquiries and exchange of information with regard to matters concerning such infringement or circumvention.

Article III

Subject to such exceptions as may be mutually agreed upon each Contracting Party shall prohibit and cooperate with the other to prevent :

1. (a) re-exports from its territory to third countries of goods imported from the other Contracting Party and products which contain materials imported from the other Contracting Party exceeding 50 per cent of the ex-factory value of such products;

2. (b) re-exports to the territory of the other Contracting Party of goods imported from third countries and of products which contain imports from third countries exceeding 50 per cent of the ex-factory value of such goods.

Article IV

Each Contracting Party will :

(a) prohibit and take appropriate measures to prevent import from the territory of the other Contracting Party of goods liable to be re-exported to third countries from its territory and the export of which from the territory of the other Contracting Party to its territory is prohibited ;

(b) In order to avoid inducement towards diversion of imported goods to the other

Contracting party, take appropriate steps through necessary provisions relating steps through necessary provisions relating to Baggage Rules, gifts and foreign exchange authorisation for the import of goods from third countries.

Article V

The Contracting parties shall compile and exchange with each other statistical and other information relating to unauthorized trade across the common border. They also agree to exchange with each other regularly the lists of goods the import and export of which are prohibited, or restricted or subject to control according to their respective laws and regulations.

Article VI

The respective heads of the Border Customs Offices of each country shall meet regularly with his counterpart of appropriate status at least once in two months alternately across the common border :

(a) to cooperate with each other in the prevention of unauthorised trade :

(b) to maintain the smooth and uninterrupted movement of goods across their territories;

(c) to render assistance in resolving administrative difficulties as may be arise at the field level.

Article VII

In order to facilitate effective and harmonious implementation of this Agreement, the Contracting Parties shall consult each other regularly.

Article VIII

This agreement shall come into force on the 6th of December 1991, and shall remain in force for a period of five years. It may be renewed for further period five years, at a time, by mutual consent, subject to such modifications as may be agreed upon.

Done in duplicate in Hindi, Nepali, and English languages, all the texts being equally authentic, at New Delhi on the 6th December 1991. In case of doubt, the English text will prevail.

(P. Chidambaram) (Gopal Man Shrestha)
For Government of India Minister of State for Commerce Nepal.

APPENDICES

Appendix X

Joint Press Statement on External Affairs Minister's visit to Nepal
July 26, 2014

1. Her Excellency Smt. Sushma Swaraj, Minister of External Affairs of the Government of India is on an official visit to Nepal on 25-27 July 2014 at the invitation of Hon'ble Mr. Mahendra Bahadur Pandey, Minister for Foreign Affairs of the Government of Nepal. The delegation includes Smt. Sujatha Singh, Foreign Secretary, Ms. Sujata Mehta, Secretary (ER&DPA) and other senior officials of the Government of India.

2. H.E. Smt. Swaraj paid courtesy calls on The Rt. Hon'ble Dr. Ram Baran Yadav, President of Nepal, The Rt. Hon'ble Mr. Sushil Koirala, Prime Minister and The Rt. Hon'ble Mr. Subash Chandra Nembang, Speaker of the Legislature-Parliament. She also met with the Leader of Opposition in the Legislature-Parliament The Hon. Pushpa Kamal Dahal 'Prachanda' and leaders of other political parties.

3. Hon. Mr. Pandey and H.E. Smt. Swaraj co-chaired the third meeting of the Joint Commission, leading their respective delegations on 26 July 2014. The meeting was held in an atmosphere of utmost cordiality and warmth. The Hon. Minister hosted a dinner in honour of H.E. Smt. Swaraj.

4. The Joint Commission was formed in 1987 at the Foreign Ministers' level with a view to strengthening understanding and promoting cooperation between the two countries for mutual benefits in the economic, trade, transit and industrial fields and in the multiple uses of water resources. Both Ministers expressed happiness at the reactivation of the Joint Commission after a gap of 23 years and underscored the importance of the Commission in furthering bilateral relations and cooperation.

5. The Foreign Minister of Nepal warmly welcomed his Indian counterpart. He thanked the visiting External Affairs Minister for accepting the

invitation and choosing Nepal as one of her early foreign trips. He stated that her visit would help further strengthen the bonds of ties between the two countries and expand and deepen the scope and dimension of cooperation. The Minister of External Affairs of India thanked The Hon. Foreign Minister of Nepal for the invitation and warm hospitality extended to her and her delegation since their arrival. She expressed that her visit to Nepal demonstrates the importance that her Government attaches to good, neighbourly relations, particularly with a friendly country like Nepal with which India shares an ancient, deep-rooted and vibrant friendship based on shared civilisational ethos. She expressed the willingness of the Government of India to explore further areas of mutual cooperation and promote partnerships, while reinvigorating the existing mechanisms for enhancing mutual benefit between the two countries.

6. Both foreign ministers shared that both countries hold similar views on major international issues affecting the developing countries and work in close coordination with each other in the United Nations and other international fora. The Nepalese side reiterated its support for India's candidature for permanent membership of the UN Security Council.

7. The Nepalese side welcomed the forthcoming visit of H.E. Narendra Modi, Prime Minister of India, to Nepal.

8. The Joint Commission reviewed the entire gamut of Nepal-India relations. It affirmed that the Joint Commission would make an important contribution to further strengthen the traditionally warm and close relations and add new dimensions in the areas of cooperation. The two leaders underlined the importance of timely meeting of the Joint Commission in the future.

9. The Joint Commission reiterated the need for reviewing, adjusting and updating the Treaty of Peace and Friendship 1950, reflecting the current realities. It directed the Foreign Secretaries to make necessary recommendations. The Joint Commission also directed the Nepal-India Boundary Working Group to commence field works at the earliest.

10. The two Ministers expressed satisfaction over the ongoing cooperation in defence sector. They expressed happiness over the ongoing cooperation between the security agencies of both countries and emphasized the need for promoting greater collaboration and cooperation in combating

Appendices

cross-border crimes. They reiterated the commitment of their respective Governments not to allow their territories to be used against each other.

11. The two sides noted the significance of enhancing productive capacity in agriculture to positively impact on livelihoods of the people. The Indian side would continue to supply chemical fertilizers to Nepal and extend cooperation for the establishment of a Deemed Agricultural University.

12. The Nepalese side appreciated India's continued technical and financial cooperation in building physical infrastructures including roads, railways and bridges.

13. The two Ministers stressed the need for further enhancing bilateral trade and investment to foster mutually beneficial economic growth and development. They noted Nepal's trade deficit with India and agreed to take effective measures to address the problem. Both sides stressed the need to complete necessary formalities to enable entry into force of the Bilateral Investment Protection and Promotion Agreement (BIPPA). In order to promote Nepal's exports to India, the Indian side agreed to further relaxing the rules of origin requirements; simplifying and streamlining transit and customs related procedures; eliminating TBT and making the SPS related measures less stringent; and lifting quantitative restrictions on the export of Nepalese products to India.

14. Both sides directed the concerned authorities to conclude pending Letters of Exchange (LOEs) at the earliest with a view to facilitating trade and traffic in transit.

15. The authorities concerned have been instructed to carry out the works of the Terai Roads under Phase I projects with utmost priority and commence the Phase II projects by concluding agreement as soon as possible. The Joint Commission agreed that the construction of Tanakpur-Mahendranagar Link Road should be expedited.It also underlined the need for expediting the construction work of the cross-border railway connectivity.

16. The Joint Commission directed the concerned authorities to accelerate the construction works in the Integrated Check Posts (ICPs) to bring them into early operation.

17. The two leaders underscored the importance of harnessing vast hydropower potentials of Nepal for mutual benefits. They directed the

concerned authorities to finalize the text of a Power Trade Agreement at the earliest. While noting the finalization of the Terms of Reference of the Pancheswar Development Authority, they directed the concerned authorities for early completion of the DPR of the Pancheshwar Multipurpose Project.

18. The Joint Commission expressed satisfaction over the implementation of 400 kV Dhalkebar-Muzaffarpur Double Circuit Cross-Border Transmission Interconnection and noted that the transmission interconnection would integrate the power grids on the two sides of the border and pave the way to initiate unfettered flow of power between the two countries. The Joint Commission decided to expedite the construction of 132 kV Kataiya-Kusaha and 132 KV Raxaul-Parwanipur Transmission Line Projects so that the transmission lines would help import additional power from India in the short term and help address power deficit situation in Nepal.

19. Both sides expressed satisfaction over the near completion of river training works over Lalbakaiya, Bagmati and Kamala. They also discussed other river training works over Dodha, West Rapti, Mohana and Lakhandehi.

20. The Joint Commission welcomed the signing of MOU on the installation of 2,700 shallow tube-wells in the terai region.

21. The Nepalese side appreciated the continued Indian cooperation in human resource development of Nepal. It welcomed India's decision to increase scholarships for Nepalese students and expressed the hope that such scholarships would be processed through Government channels.

22. The two sides discussed construction of an international cricket stadium at Pokhara and continuation of Goitre Control Programme. The Indian side agreed to arrange for necessary equipment and other assistance for an early operationalisation of the Bharat-Nepal Maitri Emergency and Trauma Centre.

23. The Nepalese side would take necessary steps for the extension of Small Development Programme, which both sides agreed to align with Nepal's development programmes and priorities. The Nepalese side would also look into the matters pertaining to benefits to the Indian teachers working in Nepal.

24. The Joint Commission noted the satisfactory progress in the projects covered under the EXIM Bank Lines of Credit (LoC). At the request of the Nepalese side, the Joint Commission acknowledged the need to relax the requirement of Indian content for the road projects included in the US$ 250 million LoC and agreed that the Indian content requirement would be reduced to 50 %. Itcalled upon the LoC Review mechanism to expedite the works of the projects identified under the US$ 250 million LoC and agreed that EXIM Bank funding could be used for bigger projects with greater socio-economic impact in future.

25. The Joint Commission appreciated the ongoing bilateral cooperation in culture and tourism sectors and agreed to further expand and deepen cooperation in these fields. It discussed the possibilities of extending cooperation for the development and conservation of Pashupati, Lumbini, Janakpur and Barahachhetra areas.

26. H.E. the External Affairs Minister of India extended an invitation to The Hon. Foreign Minister of Nepal to pay an official visit to India. The Hon. Foreign Minister of Nepal accepted it with pleasure. Dates would be worked out through diplomatic channels.

Appendix XI

Agreed Minutes of the Eleventh Meeting of the Nepal-India Joint Working Group on Border Management (Pokhara, Nepal, 10-11 February 2015)[1]

1. The eleventh meeting of the Nepal-India Joint Working Group (JWG) on Border Management was held on 10-11 February 2015 in Pokhara, Nepal. The Nepalese delegation was led by Mr. Lakshmi Prasad Dhakal, Joint Secretary, Ministry of Home Affairs, Government of Nepal. The Indian delegation was led by Shri Hitesh Kumar S Makwana, Joint Secretary, Ministry of Home Affairs, Government of India. The list of delegates and the agenda of the meeting are enclosed at Annexure-I and Annexure-II.

2. In his opening address, Mr. Lakshmi Prasad Dhakal, leader of the Nepalese delegation, warmly welcomed the Indian delegation and stated that the long-standing relations between Nepal and India are based on a shared history, culture and extensive people-to-people relationships. He expressed confidence that this meeting would further strengthen the relationship between the two countries. He underscored the need for greater bilateral cooperation in combating trans-border crimes, smuggling and terrorist activities, and for strengthening the mechanism of Border District Coordination Committee meetings to tackle and address these problems. He also appreciated the assistance of the Government of India to establish Nepal Police Academy at Panauti in Kavre district of Nepal. Furthermore, he expressed gratitude to the Government of India for providing police utility materials, training opportunities and exposure visits to the law enforcement officials of

---

[1] Source: https://www.google.com.np/search?q=Agreed+Minutes+of+the+Eleventh+M eeting+of+the+Nepal-India+Joint+Working+Group+on+Border+Management+(Pok hara%2C+Nepal%2C+10-11+February+2015)&oq=Agreed+Minutes+of+the+Elevent h+Meeting+of+the+Nepal-India+Joint+Working+Group+on+Border+Management+ (Pokhara%2C+Nepal%2C+10-11+February+2015)&aqs=chrome..69i57.5535j0j8&sou rceid=chrome&es_sm=122&ie=UTF-8

Appendices

Nepal. Condemning the terrorism in all its forms and manifestations, he emphasized that terrorism and extremism are posing serious challenges to the peace and security. He stressed on the need for close cooperation between the concerned authorities of Nepal and India to work closely in the areas of sharing real-time information on movements, financial transactions and investments of terrorists and other persons inimical to both countries' interests including those with subversive motives.

3. Mr. Dhakal stressed the need for greater cooperation, coordination to close the gaps that exist at the entry points so as to prosecute the offenders. He appreciated the Government of India for the cooperation in controlling trafficking of Nepalese migrant workers without proper documentation to the Golf countries using Indian ports of exit. He stated that the trafficking of narcotic drugs and smuggling of arms and ammunitions pose a daunting challenge to the security agencies. He reiterated the need to control the nexus of human and drug trafficking that has extended from rural to urban, urban to neighboring countries and from there to another region. He expressed satisfaction that the Border District Cooperation Committee meetings have been very useful to deal with the problems of combating trans-border crimes and stressed the need for holding BDCC meetings regularly, at least once in a quarter.

4. In his response, Shri Hitesh Kumar S Makwana, the leader of the Indian delegation extended thanks to the Nepalese side for the hospitality extended to the Indian delegation and the excellent arrangements made for the meeting. Highlighting the pre-historic dynamic relationship between Nepal and India, he said that the long-standing relations between the two countries is based on a shared, composite, tolerant culture and deep people-to-people contacts. The close relationship that we share, make security of our two countries a matter of great importance for both of us where our actions need to be in concert with each other, he said. While underscoring the need for greater cooperation between the two sides in combating trans-border crimes, smuggling and terrorist activities, he said that the Border district Coordination meetings have proved to be useful mechanism to tackle these local issues. He stressed on the inevitable need to strengthen the BDCC mechanism and ensure regular,

structured and timely meetings. Highly appreciating the efforts made by the Government of Nepal in detecting and seizing Fake Indian Currency Notes, he stressed on the need to eliminate this menace and detect and interdict the networks involved in these nefarious activities including through plugging the gaps that exist at the entry points and vigorously prosecuting the offenders. Stating that the open border poses security challenges to our peoples and countries, he said that the new and emerging threats such as terrorism, smuggling of arms/ ammunitions and trafficking of narcotics and psychotropic substances are inter-related and can be tackled through joint and cooperative efforts of the two countries. While stating that strip maps of 98% of boundary have been finalized by both the sides in the years 2005, he stressed that signing of the border strip maps for the agreed sectors will facilitate repair, maintenance and construction of boundary pillars and provide our border security agencies a modern framework for effective and efficient border management. He expressed thanks for the cooperation extended by the Nepalese authorities for the safe conduct of General Elections to the Indian Parliament in 2014 including the implementation of the code of conduct mandated by the Election Commission of India. He also said that the Indian side would be happy to address training requirements of Nepal Police and the Armed Police Force. India is committed to enhancing Nepal's own capacity in training security officials and in this regard they have assisted with the construction of the National Police Academy at Panauti, he added. Expressing concern on the slow progress on the process of setting up of four Integrated Check Posts on the Indo-Nepal border, he stressed on the need to accelerate the process. He said that India and Nepal had finalized the agreed texts of Mutual Legal Assistance Treaty and revised new Extradition Treaty in the year 2005 but both the treaties are pending for signature. He informed that the Government of India has sanctioned construction of 1377 kms of roads along the India-Nepal border on Indian side and development of around 1440 kms long road network in Terai region in Nepal as well as survey for construction of cross-border railway links at five locations on the border area are at an advanced stage. He thanked the Nepalese security agencies for providing secure environment for the construction of these projects and requested for continued cooperation in this regard. He also said the Indian side would be happy to assist the Government of Nepal in case it so desire to strengthen the immigration process.

APPENDICES

5. The two sides reviewed the implementation of decisions taken during the tenth meeting of the JWG, held in New Delhi on 15-17 January 2013, and noted the satisfactory progress made on the decisions taken therein. Both sides agreed that the JWG meetings that are held every year alternatively in Nepal and India have been institutionalized over the years and have become fruitful in border management and controlling cross-border crimes. These meetings have been important foundation for the Home Secretary and other higher level bilateral meetings.

6. Both sides agreed that the Border Districts Coordination Committee (BDCC) meetings have been useful in addressing local level problems and controlling the cross-border crimes, smuggling and terrorist activities. Both sides expressed satisfaction over the outcomes of BDCC meetings and further reiterated the need to hold regular and frequent BDCC meetings at least once a quarter.

7. Both sides agreed that enhanced level of capacity building programs for law enforcement agencies is essential in controlling the circulation of the fake currencies. It was also agreed that effective and timely information sharing needs to be further strengthened to curb the menace.

8. Both sides reiterated the need to employ strong vigilance across Nepal-India border as well as timely sharing of real-time information at various levels for combating trans-border crimes including arms smuggling, trafficking of narcotic drugs and psychotropic substances, and trafficking in person, especially women and children. Both sides agreed to enhance the level of cooperation and coordination between the law enforcement agencies of the two countries while fully utilizing the existing mechanisms.

9. The two sides agreed to strengthen measures to control the activities of the elements inimical to both counties' security interests. They agreed not to allow their territories to be used for the activities of religious or ethnic fundamentalist groups. They further agreed to exercise vigil over the activities of the elements that are inimical to the sovereignty and integrity of either of them along the Nepal-India border. They stressed the need for greater cooperation and information sharing between the relevant agencies of both countries.

10. The two sides discussed the progress on the strengthening of infrastructure at the Nepal-India border that would enhance connectivity, facilitate the movement of people/goods and bring in economic prosperity for people of both sides of the border. The Nepalese side informed that land acquisition for the border infrastructure projects has been completed, distribution of compensation is in progress and auxiliary works are being carried out.

11. Both sides agreed to further enhance the existing regular channels of communication between the police/border guarding agencies of the two countries. It was agreed that the security agencies of both the countries would continue to meet regularly to exchange information on cross-border crimes. The meeting took note with appreciation of the 2nd Nepal-India Coordination Meeting between the Armed Police Force (APF) of Nepal and the Shasastra Seema Bal (SSB) of India held in Kathmandu in December 2014 and agreed to continue such meetings regularly, at least once a year.

12. The Nepalese side expressed sincere appreciation to the Government of India for providing trainings on crime investigation including financial and cyber crimes, intelligence, traffic management, disaster management, IPS, VIP security and policing matters which have been valuable in the capacity building of the Nepal Police (NP) and APF officials. It also requested for continuation of training and provision of equipment and logistics to NP and APF. Training requirements for NP, APF, immigration and prison officials and observation tours for Chief District Officers would be duly communicated to the Indian side for their consideration.

13. Both sides noted the signing of an MOU between the Government of Nepal and the Government of India on 25 November 2014 at Kathmandu regarding the Establishment of the National Police Academy at Panauti, Kavrepalanchowk of Nepal. The Nepalese side expressed its gratitude to the Government of India for this generous support. Both sides expressed confidence that the project would be accomplished at the earliest.

14. The Nepalese side raised concern over the incidents of the Nepalese nationals being cheated by brokers in Nepal and their agents in India in the pretext of sending them to foreign countries for employment

Appendices

through India without proper visa and employment contract. It further stated that fake documents are also being produced by some unscrupulous elements in India aimed at facilitating the helpless Nepalese nationals' crossing of the Indian territory. The Nepalese side requested the Indian side to take urgent action against such elements.

15. Both sides reviewed the Nepalgunj-Rupaidiha pilot project and took note of the progress so far.

16. Discussions were held on the issues of encroachment on no-man's land and boundary pillars. Both sides agreed on the need for removing encroachment and addressing the issues of boundary pillars with priority. In this context, the two sides noted the formation of Nepal-India Boundary Working Group (BWG) in 2014 which was directed by the 3rd Meeting of the Nepal-India Joint Commission, held in Kathmandu on 25-26 July 2014, to commence its works in the fields at the earliest for the construction, restoration and repair of boundary pillars including clearance of No-man's land and all other technical tasks.

17. The Nepalese side informed about frequent complaints received regarding harassment and misbehaviors from the SSB personnel to the Nepalese people at the border and urged the Indian side to look into the matter to ensure that such incidents do not occur in future.

18. The Nepalese side stated that they have reports and information indicating significant injury or harm to the environment in the territory of Nepal due to the construction works, including roads, barrages, affluxes and embankments, carried out by the Indian side along the Nepal-India border. They raised a serious concern over imminent injury and harm to the environment from these construction works which include inundation, destruction of flora and fauna, displacement of human settlement and wetlands destruction. They requested the Indian side to consider postponing the works till a jointly worked out solution to the issue.

The Indian side stated that they

19. The Nepalese side appraised the difficulties faced by those pensioners having discrepancies in their citizenship certificates and pension documents. The Nepalese side informed that the concerned District

Administration Offices have been directed to examine and certify such cases. While appreciating the support extended by the Indian side in distribution of pension smoothly, the Nepalese side requested the Indian side to further instruct the pension authorities so that pensioners having such discrepancies will have no difficulty in receiving pension on the basis of certification by the concerned District Administration Offices. The Indian side agreed to further look into the matter and communicate it to their Ministry of Defense for necessary action.

20. The Nepalese side stated that traffic is big and roads are congested in Panitanki, Jogbani and Raxual resulting in the severe traffic jam encountered by Nepal bound containers. It requested the Indian side to consider operating bypass roads to manage smooth traffic movement.

21. Both sides agreed to recommend to their respective authorities to hold the Home Secretary-level meeting at the earliest.

22. The meeting was held in a warm and cordial atmosphere. It was agreed to hold the next JWG meeting in India at a mutually convenient date.

Signed in duplicate at Pokhara on 11 February 2015.

(Mr. Lakshmi Prasad Dhakal) (Shri Hitesh Kumar S Makwana)
Joint Secretary Joint Secretary
Ministry of Home Affairs Ministry of Home Affairs
Government of Nepal Government of India